A Study of Teaching-Learning Problems in Educational Technology

Authors

Dr. Vijaya Kumar Chavan
M.Sc., M.Ed., M.Phil., Ph.D
Assistant Professor, Department of Science & Humanities, Vignan's Foundation for Science Technology & Research, Vadlamudi, Guntur, Andhra Pradesh, India

Dr. M. Sreenivasulu
M.Sc., Ph.D.
Professor, Department of Science & Humanities, Vignan's Foundation for Science Technology & Research, Vadlamudi, Guntur, Andhra Pradesh, India

Nagendra Rao Howji
M.A., PGDTE, CELTA, (Ph.D)
Assistant Professor, Department of Science & Humanities, Vignan's Foundation for Science Technology & Research, Vadlamudi, Guntur, Andhra Pradesh, India

AkiNik Publications
New Delhi

Published By: *AkiNik Publications*

AkiNik Publications
169, C-11, Sector - 3,
Rohini, Delhi-110085, India
Toll Free (India) – 18001234070

Authors: *Dr. Vijaya Kumar Chavan, Dr. M. Sreenivasulu and Nagendra Rao Howji*

1st Edition: *2018*

Pages: *173*

ISBN: *978-93-5335-039-0*

Price: *₹645/-*

Contents

List of Tables

List of Figures

Chapter - 1

Introduction

Man has always desired for excellence. This desire has given birth to new inventions and innovations in all walks of life. Science and technology has always been instrumental in bringing efficiency and improvement in the processes and products of the human work. The world of education as also been influenced by the increased use of technology. It has provided valuable help in improving the task of the teacher, smoothening the process of teaching-learning and enriching the goals of education.

Education is a three-fold process-imparting knowledge, developing skills and inculcating proper interests, attitudes and life values. But even today, our schools are often mostly concerned with the imparting of knowledge. Today's curriculum is found to be need based. As a result of new educational aims, newer methods were designed to foster learning; and educational technology has stimulated teachers to innovate in the areas of school organization, curriculum construction and teaching methods resulting in newer concepts like "modular scheduling ","team teaching", "self-study project" etc.

Thus, educational technology means the sum total of all-educational facilities, media, methods and techniques for optimizing learning. It involves facilitation of learning through resource mobilization and utilization of learning principles.

Educational can neither be confined to the use of audio-visual aids, software materials and hardware equipment not be limited to the use of psychological principles and instructional theories for bringing imprudent in the process of teaching-learning. Being a science and technology of education, it should cover all that happens during the planning implementation and evolution of the teaching-learning process. It should devise ways and means to explore and utilize all the resources to bring improvement in the teaching–learning process. In brief, educational technology should stand for a wise application of the available human and non-human resources for providing appropriate solution to the educational problems and to improve the processes and products of education.

1.1 Technology

The simplest meaning of technology is application of scientific knowledge for practical purposes in our day to day life.

Professor G.K. Galbraith in his book new industrial state has mentioned these two characteristics of any technology.

Systematic application of scientific or other organized knowledge to practical tasks forming the division and sub division of any such task into component parts.

If any body of knowledge in education or pedagogy can meet the demands of these two criteria, we shall unhesitatingly can it "Educational Technology".

1.2 Educational Technology

According to G.O.M. Leith

Educational Technology is the application of scientific knowledge about learning and the conditions of learning, to improve the effectiveness and efficiency of teaching and learning.

According to Takshi Sakamato Bulletin of the UNESCO Regional Office for Education in Asia (September, 1971).

Educational Technology is applied for practical study which aims at maximising educational effect by "controlling" such relevant facts as educational purposes, educational content, teaching materials, educational methods, educational environment. Conduct of students, behaviour of instructors and interrelations between students and instructors".

According to W.Kenneth Richmond (The concept of Educational Technology, 1970).

Educational Technology is concerned to provide appropriately designed learning situations which holding in view the objectives of the teaching or training, bring to bear the best means of instructions.

- Educational Technology is an applied or applicational body of knowledge.
- It seeks to take help of the laws and findings of psychology, sociology, engineering and some other basic social and physical sciences.

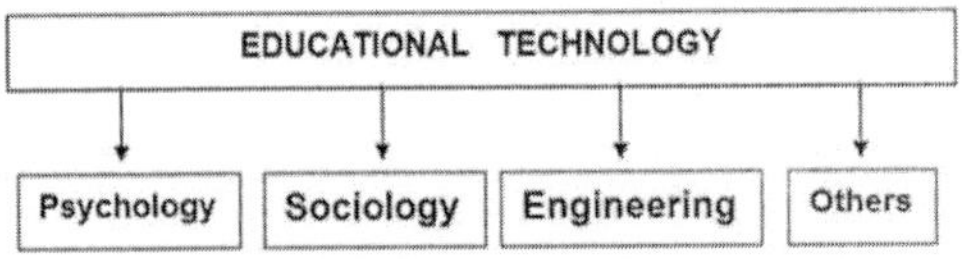

Foundations of Educational Technology

- Educational Technology aim is "to improve the effectiveness and efficiency of teaching and training".
- Leith has mentioned in his definition, or as "to improve the process of human learning", as the definition of Educational Technology given in 1967 by the National Council for Educational Technology, U.K. also emphasizes.
- It is wrong to confuse it with audio-visual teaching aids like teaching machines, T.V., Tape-recorder, radio, video-tape etc., or with programmed instruction materials. Actually, educational technology is a much wider concept or body of knowledge and audio-visual aids and programmed instruction its techniques and materials, are just some of the parts of it.

1.3 Scope of Educational Technology

Keeping an eye over such broad concept of educational technology one can be able to map out the area of its operation interns of the aspects of the covered through its study or application .

1. Analysis of the Process of Teaching-Learning

Educational technology tries to discuss the concept of teaching analysis of teaching process, variables of teaching, phases of teaching, levels of teaching, theories of teaching principles and maxims of teaching, the concept of learning, the relevance of the theories of learning, the relationship between teaching and learning, the integration of the theories and principles of teaching as well as learning for attaining optimum educational purposes.

2. Spelling out the Educational Goals or Objectives

Under this head, educational technology tries to discuss the topics like identification and educational needs and aspirations of community, survey of the resources available for the satisfaction of these needs and aspirations, spelling out of the broad educational objectives, analysis of the broad objectives in terms of the specific classroom objectives of teaching and learning, specifications of these objectives in behavioral, etc.

3. Development of the Curriculum

This aspect of educational technology is concerned with the designing of a suitable curriculum for the achievement of the stipulated objectives. It may, here describe the ways and means of the selection of suitable learning experiences or contents in a suitable frame work in order to bring out more effective instructions and thus analyzing the suitability of the curriculum in relation to the objectives, means and materials and devises of evaluation.

4. Development of Teaching-Learning Materials

Educational technology concerned with the production and development of the suitable teaching-learning material in view of the stipulated objectives deigned curriculum and available resources. Here educational technology tries to discuss the essential techniques of developing software and instructional material like programmed learning material, computer assisted learning material, mass media instruction material, personalized system of instruction, planing for the teaching and learning preparation of lesson plans etc.

5. Teacher Preparation or Teacher-Training

Teacher is a key figure in any process of teaching and learning. Educational technology, therefore, takes care of the proper preparation of the teachers for exercising their complex responsibilities. For this purpose educational technology includes the topics like models of student teaching, micro teaching, stimulated teaching, team teaching, teacher effectiveness, modification of teaching-behavior, class room interaction, interaction analysis etc.

6. Development and Selection of the Teaching-Learning Strategies and Tactics

This aspect deals with the central problem of a teaching-learning act. Here educational technology tries to describe the ways and means of discovering, selecting and developing suitable strategies and tactics of teaching in terms of the optimum learning and available teaching-learning resources; the availability of the different types of teaching methods, devices and models of teaching-their appropriate selection and use-for the optimum results.

7. Development, Selection and Use of the Appropriate Audio-Visual Aids

Teaching learning is greatly influenced and benefited through the use of appropriate audio –visual aids. Educational technology covers this aspect by discussing various types of audio-visual aids used for the educational purposes, their proper selection suiting to a particular teaching-learning situation, their development and production in view of the available resources and problems faced in a teaching-learning act, and audio-visual methods of presentation and dissemination of information, their proper storage and retrieval and consideration about their cost effectiveness and effective utilization, etc.

8. Effective Utilization of the Hardware and Mass Media

Various sophisticated instruments, equipment's, gadgets and communication devices brought through mechanization and electronics revolution are playing an effective role in the attainment of educational objectives by helping the teacher and learner in their respective roles.

Educational technology tries to describe these resources interms of their specific functions, applicability in a particular teaching- learning situation, there selection, proper handling and maintenance there preparation and development, the cost effectiveness of these equipment's and mass media in education, appropriate teaching- learning material for these appliances and the ways and means of the optimum use in formal as well as informal education to the individualized and large scale coverage situations.

9. To Provide Essential Feed-Back and Control Through Education

Educational technology is essencially concerned with the task of excercising appropriate control over the process of teaching and learning by planning and devising suitable tools and devices for the continuous evaluation of the process and products of the teaching-learning activities. Such evaluation provides an appropriate feed back to the learners as well as teachers for bringing necessary improvement at the preparatery and implumentation stages of their specific acts. For this purpose, educational technology discusses the ways and means of suitable evalution techniques, their planing, development, selection and appropriate use in relation to the objectives of teaching-learning systems.

1.4 Importance of Educational Technology

Educational Technology is of great importance to all countries because of the possibilities of its three main contributions.

Increasing the Effectiveness of Teaching-Learning Process

It seeks to increase or improve the effectiveness of teaching and learning processes. The students have been better development of their cognitive, effective, and psychomotor domains of learning.

Maximizing the Output

It enables or facilitates more learning to take place in less time by applying various empirically established generalizations from the fields of psychology, sociology, engineering and other social and physical sciences.

Enabling the Optimum use of Resources

All the countries, and especially the developing countries like India, have very limited resources in the forms of experts, sophisticated machinery or tools, time etc. Educational technology build on this very premise and tries its level best to devise new ways and means where by the teaming millions of a nation's childrens or learners may device optimum benefit from the limited resources which the nation can mobilize for educational purposes.

Educational Technology has stimulated teachers to innovate in the areas of school organization, curriculum construction and teaching methods resulting in newer concepts like "modular scheduling", "team teaching", "self-study project" etc., Thus, educational technology means the sum of all educational facilities, media, hardware and software like radio, television, films, programmed instruction, theory of learning, system approach, micro teaching and techniques for optimizing learning. It involves facilitation of learning through resource mobilization and utilization of learning principles.

Educational technology can neither be confined to the use of audio-visual aids, software materials and hardware equipment not be limited to the use of psychological principles and instructional theories for bringing imprudent in the process of teaching–learning. Being a science and technology of education, it should cover all that happens during the planning implementation and evalution of the teaching-learning process. It should devise ways and means to explore and utilize all the resources to bring improvement in the learning process. In brief, educational technology should stand for a wise application of the available human and non-human resources for providing appropriate solution to the educational problems and to improve the processes and products of education.

Learning is given more importance than teaching. The teacher has to restructure the environment for effective learning and utilize educational technology in an integrated manner.

1.5 Training Packages

Educational technology also entered the field of teacher education in many other ways for example:

- Micro-teaching procedures involve technological methods.
- Audio visual educational technology came into wider utility in teacher education programmes too. Over head projectors,film-strip

projecters, 16mm and 35mm projectors, automatic slide projectors, epidiascopes, tape recorder, charts and diagrams, etc,are also adequately used in teacher education programme to convey the learning themes to the student teachers quickly and sharply.

Hence there is an urgent need that every teacher educator in the nation is also aptly required with knowledge and skills related to educational technology. It is a must in the professional preparation of teacher.

1.6 Motion Media: A History of Classroom Use

In the first half of the 20th century, teachers were already using film in the classroom to support their lessons putting up with all its attendant difficulties, such as winding it into the projector, splicing breaks and bridging the information gaps when much-spliced films jumped haphazardly from one topic to the next. With the advent of video, this became an easier and more widespread process -although it was still necessary to search for and acquire the videos from central medial libraries and difficult to excerpt sections for targeted study or review. The ubiquitous use of motion media in the classroom was already the subject of intense research in the 1970's. Then, with the advent of streaming video, "video and web - based learning environments (became) feasible for implementation in educational settings" (Ferdig Hughes and Pearson, 1998). Today, streaming video and other education uses of the computer represent a challenging new area of study, in which researches are seeking to disconstruct the latest applications of computer-based and computer-assisted instruction (CBI and CAI, respectively) to determinate not only "what works?" but also "Under what conditions is it most effective?"

In the 1980's, when videos were in widespread classroom use, teachers reported using them across the curriculum. Films of classical novels, for example, were used to support English classes. Award-winning classic movies were put to interdisciplinary purposes incorporating political sciences, literature and media studies. Documentaries and purpose – made educational films were being used to teach history and other curriculum subjects. Writing teachers used videos by first having their students view them, then asking them to write reports, analysis are other responses to what they'd seen (Aiex, 1988).

Video continued to gain in popularity as schools increased the level of technology available in the classroom. In the mid-1990's, according to a report for the U.S. Congress office of technology assessment (Becker, 1994),

Roughly one-half of English teachers 80% of science and social studies teachers reported using 'Video, film or film strips' ones or twice a month or more. A smaller but substantial number of science and social studies teachers (but not English teachers) Reported using those media on a weekly basis – about one – third. On any given day, we estimate (from tabulations shown in the NCES code book) 5% of 10th grade in English teachers and 10% of science and social studies teachers will be using video in their teaching.

In 1998, a poll of teachers indicated their belief in the value of videos as an educational tool with 92% reporting that the use of video technology helped them to be more effective teachers and 88% that it allowed them to be more creative. At the same time 75% found that video enabled greater student understanding of the material being presented, indicating that it is especially effective with students who learn visually. The teachers also reported its self as a motivation for students who are reluctant to study, have learning disabilities or come from at risk populations (miller, 1998).

Such teacher observation has been born out by empirical study. In a research report prepared for the Bertelsmanl Foundation, Reves (1998) summarized varies findings on the use of television in the classroom, noting that "forty years of research show positive effects on learning from Television programs that are explicitly produced and used for instructional purposes" However he also points out that "Television is not widely (used) in classroom because teachers experiences difficulty in previewing videos, obtaining equipment, incorporating programs into the curriculum, and linking Television programming to assessment activities".

Of course, when watching these media, it is important for the learner to take an active role since "active, effortful processing of television results in better learning out comes than passive processing" (Bates, 2003). For this reason, one may readily infer that increasing interactive on the part of the viewer will encourage learning. A series of researchers in to the educational uses of video of also pointed out how the long established value of film, video and television to education has been enhanced by its digitization for computer access due to the potential for interactivity. (see for example, Knapp and Glenn, 1996, or Ring staff and Kelley, 2002). Recently " a report on the impact of motion media on adult and K-12 learning" (Nilankanta and Ehlinger 2003) discussed video streaming, citing a 2002 study (Boster, Meyer ,Roberto and Inge, 2002) into the effectiveness of video on demand services. The students exposed to the technology showed a 12.6% increase in achievement levels when compared with the control group.

According to the findings of some twenty years of intensive research into the marriage between technology and education, their value is not simply a matter of ease of access and use; it is far greater. Using computers in the classroom to supplement traditional instruction under teacher guidance increases both achievement and retention of content on the part of the learner (cotton, 1992).

1.7 Technology Education

Different countries use different terms to describe technology education, such as technics, design and technology, technology education, and technological education.

	Objectives	Methods	Content
SOCIETY	Technology is an integral part of society Human needs and technology are intimately Connected There is a need to establish a balance between technology and Nature There are careers in technology and the schools should provide practical, exploratory experiences related to Them	Increase cooperation between the schools and the community outside the Schools Provide experiences that prepare the student for life after school Experiences should include teamwork, analysis, invention, planning, producing, and Evaluating Experiences should be provided that promote positive attitudes toward careers in technology Experiences should be provided for all students to increase tolerance for Uncertainty For boys and girls	Systems and structures of Technology (mechanisms, Structures, products and Their applications, transfer, Storage, control, Regulation, processing, Communication, Information, energy, Power, quality) Careers in technology (production process, Working conditions, Control of quality, sharing Of work, technical Appliances used by Different professions, Changes in different Professions) Safety and ergonomics
School or College	Role of technology in Society Skill development (planning, making, knowing and understanding, evaluation, social interaction, moral and ethical) Integration with other Subjects	Integration into/with other Subjects Experiences in planning Learning by doing Teacher education and inservice development are Critical National examinations in technology are needed	Planning, making, Evaluating Information Materials Systems Control of systems Structures Processing Communication Energy and power Safety

S T U D E N T	Technological literacy (ability to use, control, and Understand technology) Problem solving skills Understanding the role of Science and technology in Society Developing technology in Balance with the Environment Moral, ethic, and social Justice Know-how, skills, values Adopting critical attitude Applications of Technology Planning and solutions From human viewpoint Students should become More innovative, Conscious, skillful, Flexible, and enterprising	Planning, co-operation and networking. Practical work: Experiments, observations and building; planning and Evaluating. Learning by doing Safety	Role of technological Development History of technology Solving technological Problems Evaluation and valuation of the relationship between humans, society, and nature Effects of technology on Nature Functions of technology (alter, store, control, and regulate) Process work (identifying, constructing, and Evaluatinwhich therefore has to be denied or ignored. Technology is around us, whether we want it or not. Thus, students should be educated to cope and deal withg) Information Energy and power Materials Safety Marketing

The way in which technology studies have been organized also differs from country to country. For the most part, technology education at the primary level is integrated with other subjects, such as handicrafts and science. Since technology education at that level is mainly taught by class teachers, it is more natural and easy to integrate it with other subjects than would be the case if the subject were taught by subject specialists.

According to Madaus and Kelleghan (1992, p. 128), a curriculum consists of six components: 1) content 2) general objectives 3) specific objectives 4) curriculum materials 5) transaction 6) results. These components served as one dimension of comparison for the study. A second dimension used three elements: rationale and content, implementation goals, and other observations.

The primary sources for curriculum information in this study were:

Australia	A statement on technology for Australian schools, A joint project of the States, Territories and the Commonwealth of Australia (Australian Education Council, 1994).
England	Design and technology in the National Curriculum 2000 (Qualifications and Curriculum Authority, 2000)
France	Noveaux programmes de 6e (Ministére de l'Education,1995) Noveaux programmes du cycle central (Ministére de l'Education, 1997)
The Netherlands	The new core objectives for the subject technology in the Netherlands (Huijs, 1997) Development of technology education (deVries, 1999)
Sweden & nbwsp;	Kursplaner för grundskolan (Utbildningsdepartement, 1994)
United States	Technology for all Americans: A rationale and structure for the study of technology (International Technology Education Association, 1996) Standards for technological literacy: Content for the study of technology (International Technology Education Association, 2000).

1.7.1 The Technology Education Curriculum of Australia

In Australia, technology is one of eight subject areas studied in schools. Technology is divided into four content areas, called strands: designing, making, and appraising; information; materials; systems. The strands are considered to be interrelated and are the basis for curriculum monitoring, revision, and reform.

Technology should be studied by both girls and boys during the compulsory years of schooling (years 1-10). Secondary school programs are more specialized, often leading to discrete programs as students progress toward year twelve. In upper secondary years, many technology programs focus on further education and life and work outside school.

1.7.2 The Technology Education Curriculum of England

The National Curriculum in England was revised in 2000 and will gradually become statutory over a three-year period. Compulsory schooling is divided into four Key Stages. Key Stage One (grades 1-2, ages 5-7) and Key Stage Two (grades 3-6, ages 8-11) concentrate on English, mathematics, science, design and technology, information and communication technology (ICT), history, geography, art and design, music, and physical education. In Key Stage Three (grades7-9, ages 11-14) and Key Stage Four (grades 10-11, ages 14-16), citizenship and modern languages are added, with one language required.

1.7.3 The Technology Education Curriculum of France

Technology education is a compulsory subject for the four years of the junior secondary level (ages 11-15). At the time of the study, there is a detailed curriculum only for class levels six (11-12 years, adaptation level), five (12-13 years, first central level), four (13-14 years, second central level) and three (14- 15 years, orientation level). A specific plan was not in place at the primary level.

Technology education aims to clarify the interconnections among work, products, and human needs, and the effects of technology on society and culture. When studying technology, pupils must face concrete situations requiring application of know-how and implementation of skills. These skills are enriched during the study process. Specifically, technology education gives pupils an opportunity to:

- Become acquainted with technical systems, their implementation and use
- Learn to use the correct language of the discipline
- Become acquainted with the special methods of technology, where a variety of solutions can be found for a specific problem
- Learn how to use developed expertise in different situations to solve a problem
- Use equipment and control systems in a rational way, by following safety precautions and the laws of ergonomics
- Observe development, different means of production, and different technical solutions to a similar technical problem
- Observe and build connections between the schools and enterprise
- Take a critical stand and participate in the technological world without emotional obstacles

1.7.4 The Technology Education Curriculum of the Netherlands

The Technology Action Plan for the Netherlands was implemented during the years 1993 to 1997 for primary schools (pupils aged 4 to 12). Financed jointly by the Ministries of Education, Culture and Science, and Economic Affairs, the purpose was to stimulate attention to technology within and outside primary schools. Importance is given to combining thinking with doing (Lemmen 1997, p. 118).

In the Netherlands, all pupils go to the comprehensive school, "Basisvorming," until the age of 15 or 16. After national debates of what the content of basic education should be, the present curriculum was published in 1998. There are at least 15 subject areas to be studied, with one of them being technology. There are five general objectives to be achieved within all the subject areas:

- Working on interdisciplinary themes
- Learning to carry out a plan and task
- Learning to learn
- Learning to communicate
- Learning to reflect on the learning process and the future

Technology is Studied from Three Different Perspectives

- Technology and society
- Technical products and systems
- Designing and making products

1.7.5 The Technology Education Curriculum of Sweden

In Sweden, the equivalent to technology education is called "teknik" (technics). According to the national curriculum of 1994, technology education aims to develop in pupils an understanding of the essence of technics, particularly, an understanding of the impact of technology on production, society, physical environment, and living conditions. Technical expertise becomes an important prerequisite for the control and use of technology.

Pupils are expected to achieve basic technical competence (grundläggande teknisk kompetens). This competence results from gaining knowledge of the role of technical development, historical perspective, and reflection on the solution of technical problems. In addition, there is need to develop an ability to analyze and value the relationships among human beings teamwork in the context of society, technics, and nature. Students are to understand the way technics is used and its effects on the environment.

1.7.6 The Technology Education Curriculum of the United States

In the United States, there are national standards for various core subjects. At the time of the study, standards existed for English, language arts, geography, music, art, social studies, foreign languages, mathematics (curriculum and evaluation standards were approved as early as 1989), and science (national standards were approved in 1996). The most recent subject for which standards were developed is technology education. They were approved at the beginning of the year 2000.

1.7.7 Educational Technology in India

Educational Technology has been increasingly used in various areas at all levels and stages of education-institutional planning, implementation and evaluation. It is used in formal as well as non-formal education.

History of school broadcasting in India dates back to January 1929 when Bombay station put out items of special interest to school children. The school TV Project was introduced in Delhi in December 1961 and now it is widely used in education. The year 1972-73 is a landmark in the history of educational technology in India. Faced with the problems of huge expansion and the need for improvement of the quality of education, the government of India launched an educational technology project in 1972-73.

The central institute of educational technology in the NCERT (National council of educational research and training) was established in 1984 by the merger of the erstwhile centre for educational technology (established in 1972-73) and Department of Teaching Aids of the NCERT. The CIET develops soft ware materials relevant to educational needs, creates competencies and trained manpower through training, conducts research and evaluation of the systems, programmes and material in educational technology. It is being funded through UNDP / UNESCO / UNICEF towards equipment.

Centres of educational technology cells/state Institutes of Technology have been established almost in all the states of India. The satellite instructional Television Experiment (SITE) was launched in the country in August 1975. INSAT (Indian National Satellite) programme was also introduced a few years ago. University Grants Commission makes use of it. National open School in Delhi was established in July 1979. Andhra Pradesh open University came into being in 1983 and Indira Gandhi National Open University (IGNOU) in 1985.

To Sum up educational technology in India is being used as under:

- School broad casts
- TV telecast lessons
- Preparation of teachers
- Distance education
- Correspondence courses
- Preparation, development and utilisation of Audio-visual material
- Language teaching.

- Production of multipurpose kits, models and other instructional material.

- CLASS (Computer Literacy and Studies Schools)

1.8 The Educational Technology Project

In 1972-73, the government of India launched an educational technology project which broadly envisages the stimulation and promotion of an integrated use of mass media and instructional technology at all levels of education. It has three main objectives:

- To bring about qualitative improvement in education
- To accelerate the rate of expansion and
- To make instruction more interesting implemented with the collabaration of UNDP, the programme involved the setting up a centre for the development of educational technology under the NCERT and development of educational technology cells in the state Department of Education and an Educational Technology unit in the Ministry of Education (Now Department of Education, Ministry of Human Resource Development, Government of India).

1.9 NCERT and Educational Technology Programmes

The NCERT (National Council of Educational Research and Training) is the main centre of activities in the field of educational technology in India. Through its departments like the Departments of educational psychology and foundation of education, the centre for educational technology since converted into central institute of educational technology (CIET) and the department of Teaching Aids the NCERT and has taken up a number of programmes. Its programmes include development of innovations in education, training of teachers, communicators and administrators, evaluation of materials and programmes and building an information bank of educational technology. It is also concerned with the development of curriculum and preparation of basic scripts for films, radio and television as well as with the production of multipurpose kits, models and other instructional material, including 16 mm films. programmes have been planned under taken by the CIET.

- The CIET has developed a multimedia package consisting of television programmes, radio programmes, activity guides, enrichment materials and tutorials for in-service training of primary teachers in science teaching. It has prepared suitable handbooks for teacher monitors as well as booklets of activities. The package was used to train 47,000 teachers during the satellite instructional television experiment.

- A survey of equipment available with educational institutions in the country for the production or use of audio-visual aid materials has been made. Nursery rhymes, collected in four languages by the Indian council for child welfare on behalf of the centre were set to music and recorded on tapes. The rhymes were translated into Devanagari and English.

- Case studies on the utilization of school broad cast programmes in Jaipur, and in Jalgaon (Maharashtra) have been done.

- A series of fifty prototype TV programmes for primary school children was chalked out by the CIET of NCERT to begin with these include eleven programmes on 'story of man' nine on 'air', six on 'National leaders of India', five on 'Delhi-capital of the country'. Four on 'world of Toys' and ten on 'food' – a total of fifty. The other three series deal with 'world of toys', 'story time' and 'Bal Jagat'. In these short programmes education content with simple messages have been selected for production. The programmes cover 5-8 and 9-11 age groups.

- Besides these, programmes which acquaint teachers of primary schools with the role and objectives of INSAT have been planned. These include role of TV in education, you and your TV set, objectives of INSAT for education and development using. TV programmes more effectively in the classroom, repair and maintenance of TV sets and evaluation of ETV programmes.

- A directory of personnel working in the field of educational technology has been prepared.

1.10 Programmes of Educational Technology (ET) Cells of States

The educational technology cells established in 21 states have increasingly involved themselves in planning educational broad casts. In several states committees have been setup to finalise the schedule for the educational programmes, and also the content. Script-writers training programmes, both for radio and television have also been organised. Teachers training programmes continue to be organised through radio and support material in several states.

1.11 Present Position of The use of Educational Technology in India

The Use Of Educational Technology in the present position in India is as follows:

1.11.1 ETV Lessons

The first school TV project was launched by all India Radio (AIR) on 2nd October 1961, with the collaboration of Directorate of Education, Delhi and the Ford Foundation. The project was taken up in 140 schools with 300 sets covering about 29,000 students. The scheme was also taken up by Doordarshan Kendras of Bombay, Madras and Srinagar.

Educational Television (ETV) in India cuts across all the levels, pre-primary, primary, secondary, higher secondary, under graduate, post graduate, and continuing. Also, it takes various forms, such as informal, non-formal and formal. Post-SITE (Satellite instructional television experiment) Educational Television programmes for children in the age ranges (5-8) years and (9-11) years developed at UDKs (Upgrah Doordarshan Kendras), namely Delhi, Cuttack, and Hyderabad and beamed for the children at Jaipur, Raipur, Muzzafarpur, Sumbalpur, Hyderabad and Gulbarga.

The central Institute of Educational Technology (CIET) and the six state institutes of educational technology (SIET) in Uttar Pradesh, Bihar, Orissa, Gujarat, Maharashtra and Andhra Pradesh provide the production facility. Since April 1988, the responsibility for programme production of ETV transmission is being shouldered by CIET and SIETs. Another important development has been that the Government has decided to make these SIETs autonomous in order to make them more professional. SIETs in U.P., Maharshtra, Orissa and Andhra Pradesh have already been conferred autonomous status. However, the working of the SIETs and the their output is still suboptimal. There is a need to improve the quality of programmes. Increasing their output has to remain a priority during the 8th plan. The programmes of an 'enrichmnet' type with the added feature that even the segments aimed at various groups of topics have not got defined. Topics get covered in a some what random manner. There would be advantage in defining before hand the optimum coverage and the objectives to be achieved by transmission of even enrichment programmes and to schedule programme production accordingly. The involvement of non-government organisations (NGOs) has not come about in any substantial manner so far.

1.11.2 Class (Computer Literacy and studies in Schools) Project

This project was initiated in 1984-85 with the objective of acquainting students and teachers with the wide range of computer applications and its potential as a learning medium. So far 2598 secondary and higher secondary schools have been covered under this scheme. A notable initiative possibly triggered by the CLASS project, has been the computer literacy programme in fees charging private schools. In most of the schools professional agencies have been contracted for providing the hardware and teaching inputs. In such cases fees are high but the outcomes are also good. The CBSE has pioneered the start of computer science at higher secondary stage and some state boards have followed this lead.

A revised CLASS project during 1993–2004 saw the introduction of PC machines in keeping with broad global trends. Subsequently, the government. Initiated the CLASS 2000 programme with the aim of providing computer literacy in 10,000 schools, computer-assisted learning in 1,000 schools, and computer-based learning in 100 schools. These 100 schools were called smart schools, and were designed to be agents of change seeking to promote the extensive use of computers in the teaching-learning process.

1.11.3 Primary Education and Teacher Training

Recognising the need to provide necessary background and orientation to primary and upper primary school teachers, inputs in educational technology have been made an integral part of in service as well as pre-service training for teachers in the DIETS. A senior lecturer and lecturer in Educational Technology are part of "the prescribed staffing norm for each DIET. These faculty members also serve as nodal points to liaise with the nearest AIR Kendra besides acting as trainers. They help them in producing educational broad casts. Teacher training institutes like DIET, CTE and IASE have been provided with VCRs and colour TVs efforts are now being made to make available adequate number of software for their optimal utlilisation.

1.11.4 Higher Education

The UGC's is country wide classroom (CWCR) programmes were started to be broadcast from August 15, 1984. the commission is at present supporting 7 educational media Research centers (EMRCs) at the University of Poona, Gujarat University (Ahmedabad), central institute of English and Foreign languages (Hyderabad), Jamia Millia Islamia (New Delhi), Jodhpur University Madurai Kamaraj University and St. Xavicr College (Calcutta), Eigh audio-visual research centres (AVRCs) at University Roorkee, Osmania University, Anna University, Madras, Kashmir University, Srinagar, Manipur University. Imphal : Panjabi University, Devi Ahilya

University, and HS Guar University are being supported for Training of Personnel and Production of software upto October, 1993 3355 programmes are produced by different media centers. Sourcewise, rearly 85 percent of the progrmmes telecast were Indian while the remaining were form foreign sources. In order to make distance learning more effective and bring best teachers in the country within the reach of all section of students including semi urban and rural students, the commission undertook a project to produce non-broad casting video lectures for under graduate students. For this, 15 subject were selected and the video course material is ready in six subjects. A TV Series comprising 13 episodes for the pre-schoolers has also been completed and shown on Door darshan. These programmes are meant to sensitise pre-schoolers with alphabets, numbers, concepts on health care sanitation, food. Various geometric shapes and the like through the medium of songs, animation, puppetry etc.

1.11.5 Educational Technology Programmes/Projects in India

Some of the major educational radio & educational television projects are discussed as hereunder:

1.11.5.1 Major Educational Radio Projects in India

School Broadcast Project

This project was commissioned in 1937 and the target group was School students. This programme started from Delhi, Calcutta, Madras and Bombay. In the beginning the school programme were not strictly governed by the curriculum. With the passages of time and acquisitions of more experience, the AIR tried to make its radio broadcasts more curriculum oriented, but in absence of common syllabi and time tables in schools, even within the same state, it could not succeed in it's aim.

Adult Education and Community Development Project (Radio Forum)

Commenced in 1956, the Villagers of 144 villages in the vicinity of Poona (in Maharastra state), were the main beneficiaries of this project. This was agriculture-based project, which was originally designed and tried out in Canada. With the help of UNESCO, it was tried in 144 villages of Poona and was named as ' Radio forums Project' (defined as a listening cum-discussion-cum-action group). The members of the forum could listen thirty-minute radio programme on some agricultural or community-development programme, then discuss and decide regarding it's adoption in their own village. This project was a great success. Many action programmes were planned and put into practice.

Farm and Home Broadcast Project

This project was commenced in 1966 and again targeted at Farmers and villagers. These broadcasts were designed to provide information and advice on agricultural and allied topics. The aim was to educate the farmers and.

University Broadcast Project

This project for University students was initiated in 1965, with an aim to expand higher education as widely as possible among the different strata of society. The Programme consisted of two types- 'General' & 'enrichment'. The general programmes included topics of public interest and enrichment programmes supported correspondence education offered by universities in their respective jurisdictions. School of Correspondence studies, University of Delhi and the Central Institute of English and Foreign Languages, Hyderabad is well known for preparation and broadcast of their programmes through AIR.

Language Learning Programme

The project, popularly known as 'Radio Pilot project' was started in 1979-80 jointly by AIR and Department of Education Government of Rajasthan, with an aim to teach Hindi to School going children as first language in 500 primary schools of Jaipur & Ajmer districts on experimental basis. The project was found useful in improving the vocabulary of children. With its success, similar project was repeated in Hoshangabad district of Madhya Pradesh with some modifications but had limited success.

Ignou-Air Broadcast

In collaboration with IGNOU, AIR stations of Mumbai, Hyderabad and Shillong started radio broadcasts of IGNOU Programmes from January 1992. Main target group of this project were students of Open / Conventional Universities. Although Shillong started this but discontinued later on. Therefore presently it is being broadcast from AIR Mumbai (Every Thursday and Saturday from 7:15AM-7:45AM) and AIR Hyderabad (Every Tuesday, Thursday & Saturday from 6:00 AM - 6:30 AM) only. This programme is still popular in the respective region.

Ignou-Air Interactive Radio Counselling (IRC)

Started in 1998 for students of Open / Conventional Universities, this project is also very successful. In order to bridge the gap between Institutions and learners by instantly responding to their queries and also to provide Academic Counselling in subject area, IGNOU in collaboration with AIR Bhopal started this project in May 1998 as an experimental programme for one year (Sharma, 2002a). With the success of the experiment, it was extended to 8 other AIR stations (Lucknow, Patna, Jaipur, Shimla, Rohtak, Jalandhra, Delhi and Jammu). Presently Interactive Radio counseling is being provided on every Sunday for one hour (4:00 PM-5:00 PM) from 186 radio stations of All India Radio. This includes two Sundays on the National hook-up. Toll-free telephone facility is available from 80 cities (effective from February 2001) enabling the learners to interact with experts and seek clarification, without paying for their telephone calls. The first and third Sundays of the month, AIR stations of Delhi (Hindi) and Kolkata (in English) broadcast from national hook-up, which 186 radio stations relay either of them. The 2nd and 4th Sunday are slotted for programmes of various regional centers of IGNOU and State Open universities respectively. The slot of 5th Sunday (if any) has also been given to region-based programmes of IGNOU. This programme is gaining popularity day by day.

Gyan-Vani (Educational FM Radio Channel of India)

This project is recently launched (in year 2001) and again the target group is students of Open/Conventional Universities. Gyan Vani (Gyan = Knowledge, Vani = aerial broadcasting) is Educational FM Radio Channel of India, a unique decentralised concept of extending mass media for education and empowerment, suited to the educational needs of the local community (Sharma, 2002b). It is operating presently through Allahabad, Banglore and, Coimbatore FM stations of India on test transmission mode. The network is slotted to expand to a total of 40 stations by June-2002. Gyan Vani stations will operate as media cooperatives, with day-to-day programmes contributed by different Educational Institutions, NGO's and national level institutions like IGNOU, NCERT, UGC, IIT, DEC etc. Each stations will have range of about 60-KM radius, covering the entire city/town plus the surrounding environs with extensive access. It serves as ideal medium addressing the local educational developmental and socio cultural needs (IGNOU, 2001).

Gyan Vani is not only for the conventional educational system but also a main tool in making available the dream of education for all come true. Gyan Vani's main intention is to take education to the doorsteps of the people. Gyan Vani, in addition to giving the hardcore education will also deal with awareness programmes including the ones for Panchayati Raj Functionaries, Women Empowerment, Consumer Rights, Human Rights, the Rights of the Child, Health Education, Science Education, Continuing Education, Extension Education, Vocational Education, Teacher Education, Non-formal Education, Adult Education, Education for the handicapped, Education for the down trodden, education for the tribals and so on. Gyan Vani is available through commercial FM radio set.

Radio-Vision (Multimedia Through Digital Radio)

Pioneered by the BBC, the technique of radio-vision allows the subject matter to be presented through two channels, the audio and the visual. The visuals are presented in the form of still filmstrips, charts, slides, models, etc, while the explanation is given through recorded narration. Educational institutions use this as a substitute for educational television. Radio-vision has its own advantages:

It is economical

- It can cater to different categories of learners
- It is easy to produce such programmes at the institutional level or at the learning centers
- It provides visual support to the concept that is taught.

A small experiment in the use of radio-vision technique was carried out by The National Council of Education Training and Research, India in 1975-76 using it as one of the components of the multi-media package for in service teacher training designed and operated during SITE. A series of charts and picture cards were presented to about 24,000 participating teachers 2400 centres alongwith verbal explanation provided through specially prepared radio broadcasts. The results were found to be encouraging. (IGNOU, 2000)

A pilot project was carried out in IGNOU in 2001 under UNESCO support for testing the feasibility of using the new digital technology for cost effective transmission of audio-visual courseware. The project proved that FM Radio transmitters and Satellite Radio transponders can be used successfully to transmit, downlink and download multimedia courseware, in this case using the Asia Star of WorldSpace (Dikshit, 2002). The details of the experiment are available at http://www.ignou.ac.in/unesco/unesco46.htm

Radio-Text

Radio has been used along with textual data transfer via computer networks simultaneously to create a 'radio-text' environment. The teaching end is normally a FM radio station having data broadcast facility through a computer network. The main points of the radio broadcast are sent through textual mode to the receiving end via a computer network. The learning end has radio listening facility as well as a computer screen to receive the textual data. Since both audio and text are broadcast simultaneously, the learner at the receiving end gets high quality and low cost teaching. An experiment on the use of radio-text at Yashwant Rao Chavan Maharashtra Open University, Nasik, India resulted in the satisfaction of more than 80 percent the learners. It also used for peer group discussion at the receiving end after the broadcast, which indicates radio-text could be used for varieties of objectives (Chaudhary, 1996).

1.11.5.2 Major Educational TV Projects in India

In India, since the inception of TV network, television has been perceived as an efficient force of education and development. With its large audience it has attracted educators as being an efficient tool for imparting education to primary, secondary and university level students. Some of the major educational television projects are discussed as hereunder:

Secondary School Television Project (1961)

This project was designed for the secondary school students of Delhi. With an aim to improve the standard of teaching in view of shortage of laboratories, space, equipment and dearth of qualified teachers in Delhi this project started on experimental basis in October 1961 for teaching of Physics, Chemistry, English and Hindi for students of Class XI. The lectures were syllabus-based and were telecasted in school hours as a part and parcel of school activities. According to Paul (1968) 'by and large, the television schools did somewhat better in the test then did the non-television schools'.

Delhi Agriculture Television (DATV) Project (Krishi Darshan) (1966)

The project named Krishi Darshan was initiated on January 26, 1966 for communicating agricultural information to the farmers on experimental basis for the 80 selected villages of Union territory of Delhi through Community viewing of television and further discussions among themselves. Experiment was successful and that there was substantial gain in the information regarding agricultural practices. (IGNOU, 2000)

Satellite Instructional Television Experiment (SITE) (1975)

This project, one of the largest techno-social experiments in human communication, was commissioned for the villagers and their Primary School going children of selected 2330 villages in six states of India. It started on August 1, 1975 for a period of one year in six states Rajasthan, Karnataka, Orissa, Bihar, Andhra Pradesh and Madhya Pradesh. The main objectives of this experiment, were to study the process of existing rural communications, the role of television as new medium of education, and the process of change brought about by the community television in the rural structure with following two type of telecast:

1. Developmental education programmes in the area of agriculture and allied subjects, health, family planning and social education, which were telecast in the evening for community viewing.
2. The school programmes of 22 ½ minutes duration each in Hindi, Kannada, Oriya and Telugu were telecast on each school day for rural primary school children of 5-12 years age group to make the children realize the importance of science in their day to day life.

SITE experiment showed that the new technology made it possible to reach number of people in the remotest areas. The role of television was appreciated and it was accepted in rural primary schools as an educational force (IGNOU, 2000).

Post-Site Project (1977)

The target group for this post SITE project was the villagers of Rajasthan. This was a SITE continuity project and was initiated in March 1977 when a terrestrial transmitter was commissioned at Jaipur. The main objectives of SITE continuity project were to:

- Familiarize the rural masses with the improved and scientific know how about farming, the use of fertilizers and the maintenance of health and hygiene.
- Bring about national and emotional integration; and
- Make rural children aware of the importance of education and healthy environment. This project was also successful.

Indian National Satellite Project (INSAT) (1982)

The prime objective of the INSAT project was aimed at making the rural masses aware of the latest developments in the areas of agricultural productivity, health and hygiene. It was initially targeted at villagers and their school going Children of selected villages in Orissa, Andhra Pradesh, Bihar, Gujrat, Maharastra and Uttar Pradesh. As a part of INSAT of Education project, ETV broadcasts were inaugurated and continued through terrestrial transmission from 15 August 1982 in Orissa and Andhra Pradesh. Later, other states namely Bihar, Gujrat, Maharashtra and Uttar Pradesh were covered under INSAT service using INSAT-1B in June 1983. In each state, a cluster of 3-4 districts were selected on the basis of backwardness of the area, availability of suitable developmental infrastructure and utilization of existing production facilities. Besides developmental programmes for community viewing, educational programmes (ETV) for two different age groups of school children (5-8 years and 9-11 years) are telecast daily. A capsule of 45 minutes duration consisting of two separate programmes - one for the lower age group and the other for the upper age group-were telecast regularly. Each programme runs for a duration of 20 minutes with five minutes change over time from one age group to the other. As of today, these ETV programmes are offered in five languages- Oriya, Telugu, Marathi, Gujarati and Hindi- for a large population of primary school children. Programmes telecast in Hindi are being received in all Hindi-speaking states in the northern belt (IGNOU, 2000).

UGC-Higher Education Television Project (HETV) (1984)

University students were the beneficiaries of this project. The University Grants Commission in collaboration with INSAT started educational television project, popularly known as 'Country wide Classroom' on August 15, 1984 with the aim to update, upgrade and enrich the quality of education while extending their reach. Under this programme, a one-hour programme in English on a variety of subjects is presented with the objective of general enrichment for undergraduates, educated public and the teachers as well. An inter-university Consortium for Education Communication (CEC) along with a chain of about 20 audio-visual media Mass Communication Research Centres were set up by the UGC at different institutions in the country, to ascertain high quality of programming for this project. Besides producing programmes at these centers, some programmes are imported from other countries, and are edited to suit the requirements of the Indian students. This project is very popular among students, teachers and other learners.

Ignou-Doordarshan Telecast (1991)

The IGNOU-Doordarshan telecast programmes, designed mainly for Distance learners started in May 1991. Initially they were telecast on Monday, Wednesday and Friday from 6.30 to 7.00 A.M through the national network of Doordarshan with an aim to provide tele-counselling to students of open universities in remote areas. Owing to the encouraging response from viewers, the frequency of this project was increased to five days a week. This programme is very popular.

Gyan-Darshan Educational Channel (2000)

Ministry of Human Resource Development, Information & Broadcasting, the Prasar Bharti and IGNOU launched Gyan Darshan (GD) jointly on 26th January 2000 as the exclusive Educational TV Channel of

India. IGNOU was given the responsibility to be the nodal agency for uplinking/ transmission. It started out as a two-hour daily test transmission channel for students of open and conventional Universities. This duration was increased in February to nine hours a day. The time slot transmission was further increased due to good response upto 16-hours by 1st June and by 1st November it turned out to be 19-hours channel. Within one year of its launching, 26th January 2001, it became non-stop daily 24 hours transmission channel for educational programmes. "The programming constitutes 23 hrs of indigenous programmes sourced from partner institutions and one hour of foreign programmes. Transmission of 12 hrs each for curriculum based and enrichment programmes is being made. The programmes of IGNOU CIET-NCERT including NOS are telecast for four hours each, IIT programmes for three hours, CEC-UGC programmes for two and a half hours and one hour each for TTTI and Adult Education." (IGNOU Profile –2002) The signal for Gyan Darshan transmission are uplinked from the Earth Station (augmented as one plus one system for redundancy) set up at IGNOU HQs New Delhi, and downlinked all over the country through INSAT 3C on C Band Transponder. Although Gyan Darshan has made its presence felt in all Open Universities and most of the prominent conventional Universities /schools, it still has the potential to reach to the door steps of learners through cable TV network. At present Gyan Darshan through the cable transmission covers about 90% in Kerala, most parts of Tamil Nadu, a few pockets in the North East, Nashik, Ahmedabad and Pune. AsiaNet has been providing it free of cost in Kerala. Efforts are being made to make Gyan Darshan available through terrestrial transmission.

1.11.6 Educational Technology Programmes in Andhra Pradesh

The following some of the Educational Technology Programmes are conducted in Andhra Pradesh.

1.11.6.1 Society for Andhra Pradesh Network (SAPNET): Mana TV

Society for Andhra Pradesh Network (SAPNET) is a major communication infrastructure initiative of the department of IT & C, Government of Andhra Pradesh. It is mandated to run 5 television channels under the name MANA TV. They are

Channel I - Higher Education

Channel II - Interactive Sessions

Channel III - Human Resource Development, Social Sector & griculture

Channel IV - School Education

Channel V - IEG Programme

Channel-1: Higher Education

Manatv started on 1 April 2002 in the premises of d Dr. BR Ambedkar Open University, Hyderabad by our central Government with the cooperation of ISRO. All Programmes related to higher education brought under the scope of Dr. BR Ambedkar Open University. This channel is utilized for distance education students and all the programmes are telecasted.

By Dr. BR Ambedkar Open University, telecasting all educational programmes to their 24 Regional centers at a time by keeping in the view of students needs.

The channel is being utilized by Board of Intermediate Education, Dr. BR Ambedkar Open University, SONET/Engineering Education, and Collegiate Education etc. for pre-recorded educational programmes transmission from Monday to Sunday, from 9am to 5pm

Tiime	Programme	Telecasting Day
Morning 9.00-9.30	Board of Intermediate	Monday to Friday
Morning 9.30-10.00	Dr. B.R.A .O.U	Monday to Sunday
Morning 10.00-10.30	Dr. B.R.A .O.U	Monday to Sunday
Morning 11.00-12.00	Technical Education(SONET)	Monday to Friday
Afternoon 12.15-1.15	Higher Education	Monday to Friday
Afternoon 1.15-1.45	Board of Intermediate	Monday to Friday
Afternoon 1.45-2.30	Higher Education	Monday to Friday
Evening 4.00-4.30	Dr. B.R.A .O.U	Monday to Sunday
Evening 4.30-5.00	Dr. B.R.A .O.U	Monday to Sunday

Channel-II: Interactive Sessions

This channel provides live interactive lectures, which allow students to view the studio-based lectures at ROT end and during the teaching session the students can call back for doubts clarification by live presenter. The channel is effectively used by the State council of educational research and Training (SCERT), Director,\Medical Education (DME), Police Department (Training Branch), Singareni Calaries Company Limited (SCCL).

The persons who wants to participate in this Interacting programme which is transmitted by the channel can dial to the following numbers 040-23551989/23553473. Toll free No:1800425-4038

Channel-III: Human Resource Development, Social Sector & Agriculture

The channel is dedicated for distance mode trainings Rajiv Vidya Mission of Primary School Education dept. Rural Development and Panchayath Raj dept. (MGNREGS), for live interactive teleconference with field functionaries for distance trainings. Social Sector–Self Help Groups/ empowerment of women (SERP), SERP- CMSA (Agriculture based prog), Women Development and Child Welfare, Public Health and Family Welfare, Adult Education, etc.

Live transmission is put out on Wednesday from 2:45pm to 3:45pm by Commissioner of Rural Development, Director, MGNREGS/EGS & Rajiv Vidya Mission/Sarva Siksha Abhiyan teleconference programme is scheduled on 3rd Friday and 3rd Saturday of each month from 10:00am to 05:00pm. SERP-CMSA programmes are schedule in 1st Saturday of every month from 2:45pm to 4:45pm. Women Development & Child Welfare Dept. programme is schedule on last Friday of every month from 2:45pm to 4:45pm.

Channel-IV: School Education

The channel is dedicated to the school education. The channel is utilized by the SCERT and SIET. The pre-recorded progrmmes are transmitted for primary and secondary schools students.The pre- Recorded lessons are prepared by best lectures or subject experts of Andhra Pradesh. By this it will be useful for rural students and those students who do not have resources. Monthly daily telecasted programme list is provided to all the schools. So that the school teacher can show these programmes to the students. By this we can rectify the doubts and at the same time and let out the creativity power.

Channel-V: IEG Programme

This channel is related to technical education students only. This channel covers Jawahar Knowledge centre Programmes and Training soft skill techniques for Engineering students.progrmmes are transmitted Monday to Saturday from 11.00am to 12.00 noon (Except Sundayand public holidays)

1.11.6.2 Siet (Andhra Pradesh): State Institute of Educational Technology

Television was first introduced in India in 1959 as a UNESCO Aided Educational Project. It was an experimental service designed to test the feasibility of using the medium as a vehicle for communication development and education. First serious effort in this direction was made under the project called SITE (Satellite Instructional Television Experiment) in 1975-76 wherein ETV received a boost unprecedented anywhere in the world. ATS-6 loaned by USA was used for one year starting from 1st August, 1975. The ground segment responsibilities were with ISRO and AIR. Communication Technology was used to reach 2,340 remote villages in 6 clusters in 20 districts spread over 6 States with a population nearly 45 millions. Andhra Pradesh was one of them. The experiment emonstrated potentiality of ETV.

With the advent of INSAT and con-comitant demand for educational media software, CIET(Central institute of Educational Technology) in NCERT (New Delhi) and SIETs in Andhra Pradesh,Uttar Pradesh,Orissa, Gujarat, Bihar and Maharashtra were established. Recent addition is Kerala.

SIET, A.P., Hyderabad was established in 1985 with 100% financial assistance from Government of India, New Delhi as a Production Centre of Educational Television and Radio Programmes in regional language (Telugu) for school children in the age group of 5 to 14.

Educational Video Programmes

The Educational Media Programmes primarily assist in the Universalization of Elementary Education (UEE). They cover a very wide area, which includes instruction in 3 R's. Programmes of immense value acts mainly as stimulants to create interest and awareness in children. Stories, Songs, Dance Ballets, Experimental Demonstrations etc., are used as formats in programme making not only develop the skills and talents in participating children, but also appeal to the viewer groups.

Through this persuasive medium of communication attempts are made to instill right attitudes and social values, which are in consonance with the needs of modern society and secular democracy. Themes like national integration, health and nutrition, sanitation, preservation of environment, energy conservation and population education are treated with over-all aim of widening the horizons.

The Institute so far has produced 2000 television programmes covering curricular and co-curricular areas, topics of general interest, both to teachers and children.

Educational Radio Programmes

In addition to the ETV programmes, the Institute so far has produced

550 Audio/Radio programmes. The All India Radio, Hyderabad allotted three days (Monday, Tuesday and Friday) in School Radio Broadcast Chunk for broadcasting SIET produced programmes. The programmes in Telugu, Environmental Studies I and II are for children for classes I to V will reach the target audience through Radio.

The Institute has also been producing Audio/Radio lessons for DPEP-SSA for broadcasting in "Vindaam-Nerchukundaam" time slot.

1.11.6.3 Vindaam-Nerchukundaam (Radio Programme)

To develop Quality in Education, SSA identified and introduced Radio lessons for primary and Upper Primary students to learn more concepts for different subjects. To achieve this concept Radio lesson scripts are prepared by expert teachers. In this scripts Burra katha, drama, humorous and wonderful stories.

According to the opinion of the students we came to know that the students highly enjoyed by listening the radio lessons and they also pleased to run the programme from the beginning of the academic year. On this result from this Academic year Radio lessons started from the month of july, on every Monday and Wednesday for III, IV and V class students Mutual Interaction Radio Information (IRI) Programme is telecasted.

S. No	Telecast Timings	Classes	Telecasting Days	Medium
1.	11am-11.45am	III, IV & V	Tuesday, Thursday	Telugu
2	11am-11.45am	Teachers	Friday	Telugu
3.	11am-11.45am	III & V	Monday, Wednesday (IRI)	Telugu (IRI)
4.	11am-11.45am	VI & VII	Monday, Tuesday and Wednesday	Telugu
5.	11am-11.45am	IV & V	Tuesday	Urdu (IRI)
6.	11am-11.45am	III, IV & V	Wednesday	Urdu

1.12 Problems In Teaching-Learning Educational Technology

The entire B.Ed Programme was fully over shadowed by criticism. The conventional classroom teaching seemed to be exactly like that of exposing a bride, newly used, to a strange audience, who neither has the familiarity of place nor the competence. So is the case of these student teachers who, when exposed to the class room of 70 0r 75, neither are capable of showing competency over the content matter not good enough in using effective, methodology of teaching. The result is disastrous indeed. The student teacher either entirely withdraws or remains frustrated on the basis of the above said facts, some of the major defects of the entire B.Ed training programmes.

1. There exists no relation ship or relevance between theoretical teaching and practical skill of teaching.
2. There is no uniformity in the programme followed in the aspects of student teaching.
3. There is clear cut evidence to say that present day teacher education is effective.
4. Teacher educationists themselves are not clear about the training objectives and evaluation procedures to show the extent of their achievement.
5. The films selected by the teachers are not in coordination with classroom teaching.
6. Lack of facilities for training student teachers in the use of the audiovisual aids.
7. Mass media by themselves cannot involve the learner and his experience actively in the learning process and do not allow him to interact with teachers and other learners in the process.
8. Linear programming make the process of learning quite dull and uninteresting on account of the following:
    a. Subject matter is broken in to very small pieces.
    b. Responding is quite mechanical and restricted.
    c. The learning process is quite slow.
9. Linear programming does not permit differentiation amongst answers, therefore, it is unable to develop discriminating power of the learners.
10. The multiple choice question provided in Branching programme may encourage guessing without under standing the subject matter of the frame.
11. The colleges of education have computers still does not have a trained teacher to operate the machine. Hence, student teachers are not in a position to programme the lessons, as they want.
12. In some of the colleges, there are such teachers who are trained only to operate the system. So they are not able to programme the lessons, as they like. Hence the student teacher also faces the problem in presenting the lesson through computers.
13. It has been found that there are students who are capable of high achievement in computer literacy but there does not exist any standard and reliable method of identifying such students.

14. Our educational system is concerned solemnly with recurring marks and our students as well as teachers both work only in that direction.
15. Some of the teachers like to make use of computers only for entertainment purpose and still some others hate the computer. They do not have any desire of bringing about any improvement in their knowledge.

1.13 Present Study

Educational technology the capacity of technology of education provides valuable help in total teaching leaving process for achieving the best possible results in an economic way through the available human and non human resources. The education commission (1964-66) her recommended that the curriculum should be in the light of fundamental objectives and preparing teachers for varied responsibilities in evolving system of education. On the basis of a task analysis and that the relationship between different subjects should be worked out so that they could be taught in the integrated manner.

In this way educational technology has been providing her worth in our country by guiding, planning, implementation and evaluating various programmes of formal as well as non formal education.

In the field of distance education, it involves the use of a combination of media for instructional purposes and provides facilities for out of school education in quite flexible way at any time in the life of a person.

Educational technology is concerned with all variables levels phases and aspects of teaching learning process. It teaches the teachers the art of teaching, the learners the science of learning.

Education Technology can neither be confined to use of teacher educator students teacher in the process of teaching learning.

To know the problems of the teacher educator and student teachers relating to teaching learning educational technology, the investigation identified the above problem for the purpose of research.

1.14 Statement of the Problem

The present investigation is concerned with the various problems that we generally come across in teaching the educational technology in B.Ed class rooms as well as the student of B.Ed programme also having the problem in learning the Educational Technology.

Some personal and demographic variables are differing in individuals in case of the teaching -learning the Educational Technology. This study also deals with the various problems in teaching – learning the Educational Technology by the teacher educators and student teachers.

The title of the present investigation is "A STUDY OF TEACHING-LEARNING PROBLEMS IN EDUCATIONAL TECHNOLOGY AT B.Ed. LEVEL".

1.15 Need And Importance of the Study

Teaching learning is greatly influenced and benefited through the use of educational technology. Teaching process is helps by various types of audio-visual aids used for educational purposes, development of suitable teaching learning material, curriculum designing, takes care of the proper preparation of the teachers for exercising their complex responsibilities (Principles, theories, levels and maxims of teaching).

In learning process students learn different theories, levels and concepts of learning through the educational technology. The present problem of research work envisages that the problems faced by the teachers as well as students in the process of teaching learning.

1.16 Objectives of the Study

The objectives of the present study are

1. To find out the difficulty level of all the teacher educators as perceived on Educational Technology.
2. To examine the problems in Educational Technology as perceived by the student teachers.
3. To find out the intensity level of all the teacher educators in Educational Technology.
4. To examine the intensity level of all the teachers in Educational Technology.
5. To find out the relation of sex, age, college, qualification, subject area, socio economic status and experience of the teacher educators on the problems in teaching in Educational Technology.
6. To find out the relation of sex, age, college, qualification, subject area and socio economic status of the student teachers on problems in learning Educational Technology.

1.17 Hypotheses to be Tested

Based on the above objectives the following hypotheses were framed

1. There would be no significant difference between the teacher educators in expressing each problem as difficulty.

2. There is no significant variation between the student teacher who feel and do not feel the problems in learning Educational Technology.
3. There would be no significant influence of some of the demographic variable namely sex, age, college, qualification, subject area, socio economic status and experience of the teacher educator on the problems in teaching Educational Technology.
4. There would be no significant influence of some of the demographic variables namely sex, age, college, qualification area, socio economic status and subject of the student teacher on the problems in learning Educational Technology.

1.18 Variables Studied

After making a careful review of the related literature and having discussions with the experts, the variables mainly relating to the problem of teaching learning Educational Technology for B.Ed students. The tentative list of the variables to be considered in this study is as follows:

1. Problems and intensity level of teaching the Educational Technology.
2. Problem and intensity level in learning the Educational Technology by the student teachers.
3. Personal variables

Table 1.1: Details of the Variables

Independent Variable	Dependent Variable
Problems of difficulty and intensity level of the Educational Technology perceived by teacher educator.	Intensity scores of the problems relating to teaching-learning Educational Technology
Problem of difficulty and intensity level of the Educational Technology perceived by the student teacher.	
Problems about the personal variables of the teacher educators.	
Problems about the personal variables of the student teachers.	

1.19 Limitations of The Study

The present study has following limitations:

1. The study is limited to the teacher educator and student teachers of B.Ed only.

2. The problem of teacher educators and students teacher are measured through the constructed problems on the Educational Technology of B.Ed syllabus.
3. This is only a precise-product study.
4. The study restricted to test the problems of teacher educators and student teacher with some demographic variable.
5. The study restricted to the college of education under the Acharya Nagarjuna University, Guntur, S.K. UNIVERSITY. Anantapur, Osmania university Hyderabad A.P jurisdiction.

1.20 Chapterization

The Thesis consists of five chapters.

Chapter II: Deals with review of related literature.

Chapter III: Deals with methodology of study.

Chapter IV: Deals with Results and discussion of the collected data.

Chapter V: Deals with Findings Conclusions and Suggestion for further Research.

Chapter - 2

Review of Related Literature

Review of related literature given on the relevant materials published in the problems are under study. The studies conducted during the last few decades in the field of problems related to teaching learning education technology that are more relevant and patient to the present investigation are discussed in this chapter.

Importance of Review of Literature

Study of the related literature is necessary for a research student to find out what has already been done in his/her problem area. "In the field of education the research worker needs to acquire, up to data information about what has been thought and done in the particular area in which he/she intends to take up a problem for Research". The published literature is a fruitful source of hypotheses of its own. It gives information about available sources and about the utilization of adequate sources. It also suggests methods of research appropriate to the problem and locates comparative data useful in the interpretation of results.

Mouley (1963) stresses the importance of review of literature in the following words. "The review of related literature promotes a greater understanding of the problem of its critical aspect and ensures the avoidance of unnecessary duplication".

By reviewing the literature, the investigator can be sure that the problem which he/she has selected does not exist in vaccum. It is a fore runner for the research worker and shows the way though which he/she should proceed.

Review of related literature widens knowledge, deepens understanding and builds up ideas and insight for better perspective and therefore is an essential aspect of research.

In this chapter, brief review of related researches have been presented to get and insight in to the present problem and also to have sound base to explain the phenomena in greater detail.

2.1 Studies on Problem Relating to Teaching-Learning Educational Technology

2.1.1 Foreign Studies Related To Learners

Bransford, J. (1986): Three general areas in which technology (microcomputers and video technology) can facilitate learning are discussed: (1) helping students develop fluency (rapid recognition of familiar patterns); (2) providing rich problem-solving contexts that invite thinking; and (3) enabling students to create products that catch the attention of their teachers and peers.

Agency for Instructional Technology (1987): Conducted on the comments and observations of the 360 students of USA and Canada on education technology. Shows as the findings of the survey of a sampling of large school districts in the United States and Canada, conducted to obtain information on the use of technology to serve students at risk of school failure.

Scardamalia, M., Bereiter, C., McLean, R., Swallow, J., & Woodruff, E. (1989): CSILE, which stands for Computer-Supported Intentional Learning Environments, is an educational knowledge media system. CSILE allows information in several media (text, drawings, graphs, timelines, etc.) to be entered into a common database where it is available to be retrieved, linked, commented on, rated, and so forth. The environments and operations of CSILE are designed to support students in more purposeful and mature, or intentional, processing of information. In this article eleven principles, based on recent cognitive research, are suggested for designing computer environments that support intentional learning. These principles include making knowledge-construction activities overt, maintaining attention to learning goals as opposed to other goals of an activity, providing process-relevant feedback, and giving students responsibility for contributing to each other's learning. Applications of these principles in CSILE are described, as well as observations from the first year of school try-out.

Bork, A. (1991): The study gets positive results Investigating whether interactive technology can improve educational systems. It describes a program to gather evidence for definitive empirical studies and discusses possibilities for establishing the pedagogical value of technology-based learning material.

Collins, A., *et al.* (1991): Conducted a researcher and three different views of students on the role of technology in assessing student performance.

Data are being collected for this project using a computer program called Physics Explorer, which provides students with a simulation environment in which they can conduct experiments to determine how different variables affect each other in a physical system.

James T.F. Poon and JJNG, (1991): conducted a study on "Students perceptions of Mathematics and design and Technology" In this paper students perceptions of Mathematics and design and technology attempts to determine students perception of mathematics and design and technology. A questionnaire was administered to a sample of 37 secondary school students who had already completed are year of design and construction studies in secondary one. The instrument measures student's perception of their teacher's influence on them in terms of interest, encouragement and confidence in their work. (Teacher Scale); and students perception of their parents encouragement, view of the subject, and emphasis on the subject (parent scale). The finding reveal that students have a more positive attitude towards mathematics and design and technology on all the three scales. The significant correlation between parent's scale and subject usefulness scale suggest strong parents influence on students perception.

Jegede, O. J. (1991): This study compared attitudes toward computer use and achievement in biology for three groups of Nigerian students (n=64): (1) working alone with computer; (2) working in groups of three on the computer; (3) and a control group that received normal instruction (lecture). Students in the second group had the highest scores on attitude. No significant differences were found in achievement.

Kulik, C., & Kulik, J. (1991): Presents a meta analysis that examines results of 254 controlled evaluation studies that compared student learning in classes taught with and without computer-based instruction (CBI). Outcome measures are described, statistical analysis and effect size are discussed, and results are reported that show that CBI usually produces positive effects on students.

Scardamalia, M., & Bereiter, C. (1991): Although adults and children both have zones of proximal development in which more knowledgeable others play essential roles, there is a difference in executive control that is most salient in question-answer dialogue. Adult learners typically ask questions based on their perceived knowledge needs, whereas with school children, questions are typically asked by the teacher, based on the teacher's perception of the child's needs. Evidence shows that children can produce and recognize educationally productive questions and can adapt them to their knowledge needs. The challenge is to design environments in which students can use such questions to guide their building of knowledge, thus assuming a higher level of agency in learning. Computer Supported Intentional Learning Environments (CSILE), a computer-supported knowledge medium designed to support intentional learning, is described, with illustrations of children's use of it in cooperative knowledge building.

Quigley, B.L., & Nyquist, J.D. (1992): Argues that video can provide effective feedback in performance courses (in speech communication) by creating opportunities for students to take the role of observer, identify and emphasize specific skills, receive feedback simultaneously with performance, and make comparisons.

Jacobson, M.J., & Levin, J.A. (1993): Education uses of networks are rapidly expanding as the problems of "ease-or-use" and "access" are gradually being solved. However, even as these problems are being solved, the solutions create second-order problems, such as students and teachers becoming overwhelmed with too much network-generated information. This paper presents conceptual frameworks that capture some of the unique properties of network learning environments, and which can be used to provide systematic guidance to the design of network learning activities and software tools to enable these activities. The authors illustrate these frameworks by showing how they have helped design two different tools for educational uses of networks, a Message Assistant and a Project-Based Learning Server.

Kromhout, O., & Butzin, S. (1993): Project CHILD (Computers Helping Instruction and Learning Development) is a computer-integrated instructional program for the elementary school. It provides for curriculum realignment and a restructured organization for the elementary school to facilitate the integration of technology into the classroom. This paper reports on a longitudinal evaluation of the effects of the program on student achievement. The effect was positive and statistically significant, across grades and schools, for the three areas measured: reading, mathematics, and total battery scores on standardized tests.

Koschmann, T. D., *et al.* (1994): In response to existing educational systems producing individuals who fail to have sound working knowledge bases, this article examines uses of technology to improve instructional methods. Reviews results of a case study that uses problem-based learning as a collaborative learning method for medical undergraduates, and presents six principles of effective learning and instruction.

Van Dusen, L., & Worthen, B. (1994): Recently, studies have been initiated to evaluate computer-based integrated learning systems (ILSs). Among those characterized by good scientific design, few have found the ILS to have positive effects on student achievement or attitudes. These findings might lead one to believe that the ILS has little impact on valued student outcomes. However, in a large national study partially reported in this chapter, it was shown that there may be another explanation for such findings, namely that in most schools ILSs are not being implemented effectively. Analyses of effects of level of implementation on outcome measures revealed that with weak implementation there is little if any positive effect of the ILS and sometimes even a negative effect, whereas with strong implementation the ILS had a positive effect on student outcomes. The authors argue that evaluation of an ILS before its implementation fully meets the vendor's implementation standards is premature at best and may seriously underestimate the potential effectiveness of the ILS. The authors suggest why school implementation of ILSs may not be optimal, and outline implications of these findings for future ILS research and evaluation. Within the individualized setting, these students manage to overcome the environmental barriers by sharing learning experiences with others and providing help to students working nearby. Within the cooperative setting, most students assisted each other in solving the problems and progressing through the program. Future research may continue to evaluate the processes and products of three-way interactions between pairs of students and a computer, in comparison with two-way interactions between a single student and a computer or within a pair of students.

Sivin-Kachala, J., & Bialo, E. R. (1994-1995): When does technology help students develop complex skills-learning that goes beyond mere rote memorization-such as the ability to write well or to engage in mathematical problem solving? Recent research points to several key factors. Technology makes a difference when the teacher has a clear vision of what students are to learn and how technology can help. Success also requires that the teacher include in his or her instructional plan ways to give students guidance in the processes and thinking strategies that make up the skill. Finally, the teacher needs to be actively involved in a variety of roles sometimes a lecturer, sometimes a coach; one day a consultant, the next day an editor.

Bernauer, J.A. (1995): Integrating technology into the curriculum. First year evaluation. A program for infusing technology into the high school curriculum was initiated with grant funds at the Western Pennsylvania

School for the Deaf in 1993-94. Evaluation results were generally positive in terms of measured student and teacher outcomes and extremely positive in terms of the development of and capacity for delivering the technology-infused curriculum. The most important result may have been student enthusiasm for the technology.

Haugland, S. (1995): Examines the factors contributing to the progression of microcomputers into the early childhood classroom. Suggests that inevitable changes in the character of early childhood education caused by technology will, in fact, be positive changes.

Jonassen, D.H. (1995): Cognitive tools, computer-based applications normally used as productivity software, can also function as knowledge representation formalisms that require learners to think critically. Databases, spreadsheets,semantic networks, expert systems, and multimedia/hypermedia construction can function as computer-based cognitive tools to expand student thinking, changing the college student's role to that of knowledge constructor rather than information reproducer.

Butzin, S.M. (1997): This paper discusses Project CHILD (Computers Helping Instruction and Learning Development), a program promoting active learning and the integration of technology with learning stations. First piloted in Florida in 1991 and adopted by 57 schools, the project's success has been ensured by documentation, updates, encouragement, and support. It also describes a day in the life of a Project CHILD fourth grader.

Follansbee, S., *et al.* (1997): Describes a 1995-96 CAST (Center for Applied Special Technology) controlled study conducted in seven major U.S. cities that measured the effects of online usage (via Internet and Scholastic Network) on student learning. Results show that online use can increase student performance. Students in experimental classes produced better results on a civil rights unit than those in control classes.

Jackson, D., *et al.* (1997): Reports on a study that examines the experiences of six teachers at three schools in learning about and beginning to implement or enhance project-based learning in their middle school science classrooms using a variety of resources available on the Internet.

Marx, R.W., *et al.* (1997): Discusses changes in ideas about learning underlying reforms in science education. Highlights experiences with project-based science, which focuses on student-designed inquiry organized by investigations to answer driving questions, including collaboration among learners, new technology, and the creation of authentic artifacts that represent student understanding. Illustrates challenges of project-based science for classroom practice, professional development, and policy.

Riffel, J., & Levin, B. (1997): Discusses school responses to changes in information technology, based on survey data and case studies of four school districts in Manitoba, Canada. Financial, administrative, and political issues appear to have dominated the agenda. Debates over priorities, costs, and expectations of teachers have been central. Information technology has not yet been integrated into people's thinking about teaching and learning. Sample of the Study: The sampling technique employed for the study is quite appealing. In all 150 students of Pratom-3 and 150 students of Pratom-6 belonging to Buriram Province participated in the study.

Secules, T., *et al.* (1997): Students participating in the technology-rich Schools for Thought program learn to acquire, evaluate, organize, and interpret information and communicate findings to their peers and to an adult, questioning audience. Evolving from three research-based programs, Schools For Thought features a rigorous, standards-based curriculum; careful content/process integration; feedback from many sources; authentic use of technology; and an inclusive learning community.

McKenzie, J. (1998): The wired classroom: Creating technology enhanced student-centered learning environments. This article defines the kinds of wired classrooms, which would make a huge capital investment in networks worthwhile and also thus the results that the students central learning environment enhanced with wired classroom.

O'Hagan (1999): suggests that educational technology can be used to present and provide content, assess students learning, provide feedback, scaffold student learning and enable peer-to-peer collaborative learning.

Albion, (2000); Watson, Proctor, Finger and Lang, (2004); and Steketee, (2005): The literature on the integration of ICT into teacher education in Australia, UK and USA has focused on students' acquired ICT knowledge and skills and their ability to transfer these skills to classrooms. The available literature suggests that separate ICT units with a focus on the development of computing skills do not necessarily lead to their transfer to the classroom.

Eggleston, (2000), Atkinson (2000) AND Elmer (2002): laments the peripheral status of meta-cognition in the D&T literature. Results of a relatively small study of 27 pupils taking GCSE suggest that D&T is not capitalizing on its potential for pupil learning because of the need for high levels of performance at public examinations which fail to reward creativity found. Opportunities for pupils to develop their high order thinking skills (e.g., creative thinking, critical thinking, analytical thinking) and problem-solving skills which they will need to participate in our technological society.

Mc Kenzee, Frank Hubert, Mc Auleng (2000): Explored the link between educational technology utilization and students achievement and also a positive relationship between educational technology utilization and improved students learning based on 12 grade students and teachers perceptions and found the significant relationship between educational technology utilization and also a positive relationship between educational technology utilization and improved students learning based on 12 grade students and teachers perceptions.

Kay Stables and Richard Kimbell (2001): Reports on the evaluation of a three-year curriculum initiative introducing technology education through a learner-centered, problem solving and collaborative approach. Draws attention to the critical impact the project had on the pedagogy of teachers. (DDR)

Broere, H. C. Geyser and M. Kruger (2002): Discusses the enhancement of higher education in South Africa through technology, exploring some relevant aspects through learner-centered and managerial perspectives. Outlines some critical conditions to integrate technologies into teaching and learning. (SLD)

Cameron Richards (2002): Part of a special section on e-learning prospective in the Asia-Pacific region. The writer discusses, in an Australian context, an integrated rather than add-on model of e-learning convergences. This model applies to both distance education and on-campus online courses, reflects the use of information and communication technologies as an extended new literacy rather than discrete set of skills or information in a vacuum, and represents a new educational paradigm that builds upon, but goes beyond, a constructivist perspective in the academic and commercial sphere. It involves an approach that encompasses both appropriate and effective learning environments and activities and the interplay of social knowledge and individual performance grounded in specific and concrete contexts.

Mandi Axmann, Wiida Fourie and William Duncan Papo (2002): Discussion of online learning focuses on course development at a South African residential institution that incorporated online assignments into a face-to-face journalism course to introduce information technology. Describes course structure, activities, assessment methods, student involvement, and problems with students' lack of computer skills and access to personal computers and the Internet. (LRW)

Jean Chen (2003): Educational Technology in Introductory College Physics Teaching and Learning:The Importance of Students' Perception and Performance"In this paper the researcher explored how introductory physics student perceptions about learning physics and their perspectives about physics instructors' presentational formats might be developed. Within a Constructivist framework, it is of fundamental importance that the educators understand and addres sstudent expectations about effective instructional methods and educational technology-integrated Curricula in particular. The researcher also investigated the likely impact of student expectations of learning outcomes as part of the implications of improving the approach towards teaching.

John G. Hedberg and Lim Cher Ping (2004): Numerous schools in Asia are implementing innovative strategies to ensure the success of electronic learning. Three issues that are critically important for the success of these initiatives relate to the design of learning tasks, support and resources in the learning environment, and reorganization of methods of communication. Each of these potential challenges is discussed. John Eggleston. Forging ahead. Botswana is leading the way in design and technology education in southern Africa, with a wellestablished and highly developed program in its senior secondary schools and a newly introduced mandatory three-year program for junior secondary schools. The subject enjoys a level of resourcing that is the envy of many other countries. In contrast to the situation in Great Britain, there has been no attempt to erase the country's tradition of skills.

William Horton and Katherine Horton (2003): A comprehensive guide to help you cut through the hype in order to select the best E-Learning tools and vendors for your specific needs. With its ability to both reduce operating costs and train more people, ELearning is an attractive option for companies that are trying to balance business and educational goals. But in order to implement an E-Learning program, you'll have to wade through hundreds of learning management systems, learning content management systems, authoring schools, and collaboration environments to determine what solution will work best for your situation. In this in-depth book, recognized E-Learning experts William and Katherine Horton survey the entire field of E-Learning tools for you. They provide you with a systematic way to identify, evaluate, and choose products and services based on different E-Learning scenarios.

Elijah I. Omwenga (2004): A UNESCO/ANSTI sponsored study to carry out a needs assessment of five Universities in East Africain order to determine their state of readiness to embrace ICT and educational technology. The paperreports on students' access to computer facilities, the percentage of staff with computers in the offices;the networking of computers in the faculties of science and engineering, nature of link with the Internet, general computer literacy of staff and students and factors that affect the use of ICT as an educational technology. It also determines in each university the resources (both human and material) required to enable the institution to use ICT as an educational technology; indicates the resources required for each level of use of ICT as an educational technology and the level of within classroom interaction, at the level of interaction within departments, faculty and campus and the level of interaction with the wider world. The objective of the report is also to establish training needs for the use of ICT in science and engineering education.

Philip Uys (2004): Networked educational management has emerged as an effective, distributed management approach for managing educational technologies and e-learning in educational institutions. This management model has been developed during the writer's doctorate research and implementation of e-learning (also referred to as networked education) at Massey University, New Zealand, as well as on consulting assignments over the last six years including a five-month consulting engagement at Cape Technikon, South Africa. Networked educational management has found its widest syntagmatic expression or manifestation at the University of Botswana where the writer has been leading the university-wide implementation of modern educational technologies and e-learning since early 2001. This paper describes this syntagm or practical e-Learning and Application of Educational Technology in African countries, or in Contexts Relevant to Africa manifestation of networked educational management and concludes that networked educational management, as a new educational management paradigm, has promising features for addressing the need for client satisfaction within higher education while also ensuring that strategic imperatives of the institution are being fulfilled

Adeline Du Toit and Marie-Luce Muller (2005): Internet and Web-based hardware and software are being developed and supported on an international scale. The Department of Information and Knowledge Management at the University of Johannesburg, in cooperation with IBIS

Business and Information Services, presented the first-ever course in South Africa on competitive intelligence analysis in 2003. The short course in Strategic Competitive Analysis is described as an example of a successful Web-based distance learning programme.

Fresen. J.W. and Boyd. L.G. (2005): This study investigates the quality assurance of web-supported learning and may be considered a selfevaluation exercise of the e-learning design and production unit at the University of Pretoria, South Africa. While the 'quality' discourse and the 'e-learning' discourse are topical, there is little evidence of research projects which attempt to diminish the gap between them (Reid, 2003). The theoretical framework on which this study is based is that of an integrated, process-based quality management system, applied to web-supported processes and products. The paper is presented in three parts, namely the methodology of the quality management system, critical success factors for web-supported learning, and a student feedback survey measuring client satisfaction.

Henning Patzold (2005): The writer describes an e-learning offering that was implemented at low cost in a general pedagogy course at the Technical University of Kaiserslautern, Germany. The course involved a blended learning format to allow discussions to be added to the lecture. The e-learning element of the course aimed to give students an opportunity to deal with the concepts mentioned in the lecture and the literature through online chats and forum discussions and to offer students a way to prepare better for the examination by creating such resources as online quizzes and lists of central concepts. Overall, the online activities proved of benefit to the students and the teachers, with students who made extensive use of the online material performing better in the examination and teachers becoming more precise in their planning and gaining an additional way to estimate how competent students make use of the concepts taught in the lecture.

Bassoppo-Moyo and C. Temba. (2006): This paper examines eLearning from three related perspectives, two of which address the planning and administration of online courses. The second part of this paper examines the assessment and evaluation of learning outcomes in an eLearning environment. The initial phase thoroughly explores current and recommended front-end approaches to improving online instruction. It looks at the organizational alms and the vision within which eLearning can be applied. The second phase examines the planning, implementation and administration of online courses. It investigates characteristics of effective eLearning environments that address physical, technical, pedagogical, professional and environmental elements. The third and final phase explores several reliable and valid approaches to online measurement and testing methods that are designed to eliminate such problems as plagiarism, technical problems associated with access, matching learners' and instructors' technical skill levels, learner isolation, and the impersonality of computerized assessment.e-Learning and Application of Educational Technology in African Countries, or in Contexts Relevant to Africa technologies (ICTs) into learning.

Carol K.K. Chan and Ming Fai Pang (2006): Part of a special issue on teacher collaboration in learning communities. An introduction to the special issue is provided. This special issue addresses the teacher learning issue in light of current changes in technological, socioeconomic, and educational contexts worldwide, with particular emphasis on the Asia-Pacific region. Specifically, it explores how to use teacher collaboration in learning communities to prepare teachers to face the challenges of this new era.e-Learning and Application of Educational Technology in African Countries, or in Contexts Relevant to Africa.

2.1.2 Foreign Studies Related To Teachers

Leary's (1957) in his interpersonal behavior model, in which teacher behavior is "mapped with the help of a proximity dimension (Cooperation-Opposition) and an influence dimension (Domination-Submission)".

Brophy, (1985), Sadker, Sadker, & Klein (1991): Conducted a research amd interaction of male and female teachers. He reported on teachers interactions with students males were found to get more attntion than did females. An important factor influencing classroom interaction, in addition to student gender and academic standing, is the style of communication of the teacher.

Cradler, J, & Bridgforth, E. (1996): They did a work on recent research on the effects of technology on teaching and learning. Explains with the results the benefits and the most appropriate uses of technology and telecommunications to support and expand teaching and learning.

Kulik, J., *et al.* (1985): Effectiveness of computer-based education in elementary schools. Studies shows that computer-based education has generally had positive effects on the achievement of elementary school pupils. However, these effects are different for off-line computer managed instruction and interactive computer assisted instruction (CAI); interactive CAI produces greater increases in student achievement scores.

Vanderveken, 1985; Eemeren & Grootendorst, 1984; Ramirez, (1988), Jackson, (1968): Made a research on the study of teacher-student classroom interaction. Teacher-student interaction, by its very nature, can be characterized as a systematic and intensive social contact, necessitating a mechanism that maintains order and contro. The variables associated with the process of classroom interaction are determined by school roles and the structure of the lesson itself.

International Technology Education Association (1989): Technology education in action: Outstanding programs. This report discusses the need to restructure learning environments to support the active use of technology by teachers. The teaching learning may improve when using education technology in the schools.

Niemiec, R.P., *et al.* (1989): Compares the effects of peer tutoring and computer-based instruction on student achievement and motivation through a meta-analysis of research. Cost effectiveness is also investigated via ratios which combine the effects of the intervention with estimates of implementation costs, and an appendix includes reviews of 10 cost-effectiveness research studies.

Dwyer, D.C., *et al.* (1990): The evolution of teachers' instructional beliefs and practices in high-access-to-technology classrooms. Paper presented at the annual meeting of the American Education Research Association, Boston, MA. It gives that the instruction itself and practices highly assessed with teaching classroom.

Kerr, S.T. (1991): Describes educational technology's place in classroom teachers' thoughts and practices, examining three assumptions (teaching and teachers, what technology contributes to instruction, and how technology is used). Information is presented from two studies of teachers' classroom practice and technology's place. Implications of changes in practice to improve teacher education are noted.

Novak, D.I., & Knowles, J.G. (1991): Describes a study that explored the instructional use of computers by beginning teachers, specifically the ways in which they used the computer, the influences on these uses, and the impact of these uses on their teaching and socialization into the profession.

Oakland County (MI) Schools. (1991): Teaching and learning with technology Results of comparisons between treatment and control classrooms indicated that the classrooms differed in the amount of technology available, number of technologies used, and ways in which technology was used to meet curricular objectives. The overall results of the experimental program were favorable. Pupils are able to design, make, and appraise new artefacts and systems. Pupils are able to diagnose and rectify faults in artefacts and systems.Pupils are able to improve and extend the uses of existing artefacts and systems. Pupils are able to make critical appraisals of the personal, social, economic, and environmental implications of artefacts and systems. Pupils are able to use existing artefacts and systems effectively.

Poirot, J.L. (1992): Discussion of the assessment and evaluation of educational technology focuses on appropriate research methodologies for use by elementary and secondary education teachers. Distinctions between assessment and evaluation are explained; the need for adequate planning is discussed; student benefits and attitudes are considered; and teacher needs and attitudes are addressed.

Poirot, J.L., & Knezek, G.A. (1992): This third in a series of articles on work conducted at the Texas Center for Educational Technology and the University of North Texas focuses on research designs for teachers to determine the impact of technology in the classroom. Highlights include research and the scientific method, qualitative versus quantitative research; and statistical inference. Population & Sample : Sample of ETV Programme: Six ETV programmes for class VIII, produced and telecast by the SIET, Orrisa, Bhubaneshwar were selected, namely, The Living Fossils, Composition of water, The environment, Properties of water, The Dust particles, and Thermal expansion of matter. Intact classroom groups were used as the sample groups (composition of sample students from rural and urban background was deliberately manipulated to ensure a fine dispersal of TLP) the number of students for difference ETV was different and ranged from 155-170. Findings: Children's learning through the ETV programmes was found to be positively influenced by their Television Language Proficiency. The Television viewing strategies, namely, Direct Viewing, Viewing with Note taking, and Advance Organizer followed by Viewing produced similar influences on cognitive map formation among the learners. The ideal cognitive maps of the sample ETV were transacted more at the concept level than at the Proposition Level. In most cases distorted transaction of the message items was more than the meaningful transaction. Learners cognitive maps contained large amount of feeble and blurred concepts and proposition, chiefly inadequate Learning, idiosyncrasies, confusion, some amount of over-learning and marginal overgeneralization. Meaningful and distorted transaction of the concepts and propositions exhibited distractive relations with message type, message form and message track. These basic relations could be instrumental for improving educational tele-production and to make TV a more potential institutional medium. The study further sensed possibilities of relationship among cognitive mapping, the said production variables and tele-instruction strategies which need further probing. This is felt that tele-visual instructional designs in general and the process of message mediation in particular need reexamination for effective education of children.

Bracey, G. (1993): It shows that 1) teachers with computers expect more from their students and spend more time with individual students; 2) teachers save an average of 36 minutes a day in administrative tasks alone; 3) citations to three studies about teachers and computing.

Adriano, C.T., & Shrock, S.A. (1994): conducted to identify specific variables that contributed significantly to teacher competence, affect familiarity, and perceived skill of Philippine school students. Four independent variables were analyzed: place of work. Findings suggest specific variables significant in designing a curriculum for preparing teachers in implementing educational programs. The results of the competence test of this study imply a need for training in the use of instructional design and in the instructional technology field.

Davidson, G.V., & Ritchie, S.D. (1994): Conducted a survey on How attitudes of parents, teachers, and students toward computers affect the integration and use of computer technology in schools was studied at an elementary school in Texas. The study involved 475 students, 34 teachers, and 230 parents in two school years. Measurement indicated that attitudes improved or increased in the second year. The technology less apparent, but results tend to confirm the belief that successful implementation of technology requires a supportive environment from administrators and the community.

Abbas. Z.W. (1995): In this study on "Attitude towards using computers among Malaysian teacher education students" found that teacher attitudes have been found to be a major predictor of the use of new technologies in instructional settings

Baenen, N., *et al.* (1995): On the students during 1993-94 and 1994-95, eight Wake County (North Carolina) Public School. This report summarizes the status of the participating schools. Results include (1) A variety of technology components were implemented in all MSAP schools. Instructional Technology Resource Teachers (ITRTs) conducted many types of training and served as resources to help teachers use technology in their classrooms in all subjects; (2) Teachers believe integrating technology with their teaching is important, but many reported that before MSAP, they did not use technology because of time constraints and curriculum coverage requirements.

Bialo, E., & Sivin-Kachala, J. (1995): Effectiveness of technology in schools in USA. The results gives that Washington, DC: Software Publishers Association. The using technology to support instruction improved student outcomes in language arts, math, social studies, and science.

Ely, D.P., *et al.* (1995): Trends in educational technology A comparison of the findings from 1995 to other trend studies by the author conducted in 1988, 1989, and 1991 provide readers a longitudinal perspective on trends. Identifies and discusses eight current trends in this growing field: computers in schools, networking, television in the school, advocacy for educational technology, educational technology in the community, new delivery systems for educational technology, technological literacy for teachers, and educational technology and educational reform. Ethnographic study. For phase-2, that is, survey study a total of 30 secondary schools, 10 each from the three types were selected. 300 teachers was selected, 100 from each of CBSE, ICSE and SSC. The data were analyzed through frequencies, % responses, crosstabulations, Binomial test, skewness and kurtosis.The study has come out with meaningful finding as follows: A large majority of the Principals and Teachers were found to have high level of satisfaction with respect to Intel Training to Teachers on MS Word and MS Power Point, whereas, the level of satisfaction with respect to the MS Publisher was found relatively low. SSC teachers were found to have higher level of satisfaction than that of the ICSE and CBSE. Teachers having Teaching Experience >10 years & <20 years were found to higher level of satisfaction than those having < 5years, >5 years & <10 years, and >20 years. Master Trainers were found to have Higher level of satisfaction than the Beginners. Higher the access to internet and computer at home and School higher was found the level of satisfaction. Teachers having moderate commitment were found to have higher level of satisfaction than those having high or low levels of commitment. A large majority (>=90%) of the selected Principals and Master Trainers showed a low extent of application of MS Publisher. A majority of the Principals and Teachers observed a high extent of application (browsing) of the Internet by the teachers for information / graphic / maps. A majority of the Principals and Teachers observed a high extent of application of requiring technical support by the

Teachers when working on the computer. CBSE teachers were found to have higher level of application of the Intel's Training Program than the ICSE and SSC teachers. Teachers having Teaching Experience < 5 years were found to higher level of application of Intel's Training Program than those having < 5years, >5 years & <10 years, >10 years & <20 and >20 years teaching experience. Master Trainers were found to have Higher level of Intel's Training Program than the Beginners. Higher the access to internet and computer at home and School higher is the level of application of Intel's Teach to the Future Program. Teachers having high commitment were found to have higher level of application of the Intel's Training Program than those having low or moderate levels of commitment. Teachers having a Special Time-Table were found to have higher level of application of Intel's Training Program. Both the Principals and Teachers were found to believe that computer technology is a powerful tool for helping teachers improve student learning. Findings of the Study are the study has resulted in the development of CAI Programmes on selected five units of Thai language both for Pratom-3 and Pratom-6. The CAI Packages developed by the investigator on Thai language have been found effective at both the levels, that is, Pratom-3 and Pratom-6 as evident through the t-values with the students of Buriram Kindergarten with Experimental Groups 1 and 2. The CAI Packages developed by the ONPEC on English language have been found effective at both the levels, that is, Pratom-3 and Pratom-6 as evident through the t-values with the students of Buriram Kindergarten with Experimental Groups 1 and 2. The CAI Packages developed by the investigator on Thai language and ONPEC on English language have been found equally effective at both the levels in Buriram Kindergarten. The CAI Packages developed by the investigator on Thai language and by the ONPEC on English language were found significantly and equally effective with all the eight replication groups. The CAI Packages developed by the investigator on Thai language and by the ONPEC on English language received favourable opinions both by the teachers and students.

The State of the Art of Distance Education in SEAMEO Member Countries (1995): e-Learning and Application of Educational Technology in African Countries, or in Contexts Relevant to Africa Discusses the distance education programs of nine SEAMEO (Southeast Asia Ministers of Education Organization) countries. Highlights include technological advances and technology needs; educational reform; formal and nonformal education; educational resource centers; educational media including print materials, broadcast media, and audiovisual materials; open universities;

elementary, secondary, and higher education; and program developments and problems. (AEF)

Cradler, J. (1996): Implementing technology in education: Recent findings from research and evaluation studies. The findings of studies related to technology implementation. The suggested approach emphasizes instructional and student needs first and then thorough planning to integrate technology in ways that enhance and extend instructional and learning opportunities.

Ediger, (1996): conducted a study of Education in technology . He found that Promoters of computers use in the classroom claim that exposing pupils to web sites, e-mail and new groups promises more than the means to securing a job in the next century. Technology booster also predict that the use and mastery of the internet out world wide web (www) will produce affective changes that can be measured to produce increased students self esteem and confidence. Whether working at home or at school, as an individual or in cooperative learning or team setting, students will become infotectives, i.e., Independent thinker's, researchers, inventors, inquirers, capable of solving problems that often require the active direction of a teacher or superior.

Moersch, C. (1996-97): If technology is to have more than a modest impact on curriculum design, educators must embrace a new paradigm integrating technology in the classroom. Describes LoTi (levels. of technology implementation), an instrument to measure the degree to which computers are used to support concept-based or process-based instruction, consequential learning, and higher order thinking skills.

Advanced Technology Group. (1997): Full-text online reports summarize research (done by Apple or others) on the effectiveness of technology in language arts, math, science, reading and writing, social studies, management and administration, and preparing students for the workplace.

Barowy, B. & Laserna, C. (1997): This article describes a project that explores the combined use of Internet client-server technology and interactive computer modeling software for improving secondary science teaching. Classroom core practices are evaluated for traceable impacts of change in student learning.

Grassl, R., & Mingus, T. (1997): During the summer of 1996, at the University of Northern Colorado, we taught a problem solving course to twenty secondary mathematics teachers. Our goals in the course included promoting the NCTM Standards regarding problem solving, discussing alternative assessment, implementing appropriate use of technology, and learning content while engaged in a cooperative learning mode. In allowing them to probe on their own, technology became a means for them to develop as teachers and as problem solvers.

Mergendoller, J.R. (1997): Research suggests that technology is an equivocal blessing. Although it expedites our ability to access, share, manipulate, and display information, it provides little or no guidance regarding the quality, relevance, or timeliness of the information it processes. Teachers must take this responsibility and help students develop their own information discrimination skills.

Mc Cracken (2000): Design as "the creative soul of technology". As a human soul is to the body, design is to technology. Like the inseparable relationship between body and soul, technology is incomplete without design. Design cannot be fully appreciated without an understanding of technology.

Sunderberg, Cheryl White (2000): Studied impact of different communication technology to support professional development of teaching science. The researcher found E – Mail was the prefered mode for follow-up to on site workshops and E-mail was the most convinient and efficient way to follow up onsite.

Wulf (ITEA, 2000): Emphasized the importance of edcuational technology K-12 classroom in America". He started that Technological design is a distinctive process with a number of defining characteristics: it is purposeful; it is based on certain requirements; it is systematic, it is iterative; it is creative; and there are many possible solutions. These fundamental attributes are central to the design and development of any product or system, from primitive flint knives to sophisticated computer chips.

Kimbell & Perry, (2001): suggest that use of design and technology as a unitary concept is intended to emphasize the intimate connection between the two activities as well as to imply a concept which is broader than either design or technology individually and the whole of which we believe is educationally important it is clear that:

Knapper (2001): Technology may be a good solution for some instructional problems, and in some cases it may be a partial solution. But in other instances technology does little to address the fundamental teaching and learning issue or even worse provides a glitzy but inappropriate solution to a problem that has simply been misconstrued.

Wagner, 2001; Garrison & Anderson, (2003): Department of Education (2001):developing the kind of graduates and citizens required in an information society; improving educational outcomes (especially pass rates) and enhancing and improving the quality of teaching and learning.

Baylor. A and Ritchie. D (2002): Reported that regardless of the amount of technology and its sophistication, technology would not be used unless teachers have the skills, knowledge and attitude necessary to infuse it into the curriculum.

Edward L. Meyen, Ron Aust and John M. Gauch. (2002): The Internet and its applications in education and industry have significantly influenced how we teach and learn. This has all occurred as a consequence of emerging technologies and the demands for online instruction by consumers. In the midst of this environment of rapid growth, a new form of pedagogy has emerged. However, much of it is not the result of research. This paper addresses the need for a conceptual approach to researching, e-learning instructional design and the technologies employed as a basis for e-learning. A programmatic research construct is offered as a structure for building a conceptual model. Three categories of variables are considered in building the construct. They include outcome, in situ, and independent variables. The intent of the paper is to engage researchers and developers in a process of further defining the variables and translating them into research questions that might serve as guidelines in building the literature base for the pedagogy of online instruction.

Flecknoe, (2002); McCormick and Scrimshaw, (2001): It has been suggested that information and communication technologies (ICTs) can and do play a number of roles in education. These include providing a catalyst for rethinking teaching practice.

Joy, B.H.H. and Manickam L.S.S. (2002): Conducted a study on" computer – Assisted Instruction." They found that there was no significant difference on the teacher competency in the pre and post scores or between the experimental and control group but teacher competency was positively related to post knowledge in CAI of the experimental group. There was significant difference between the groups in their attitude towards computer education. As a result of training in computer assisted instruction (CAI), the attitude of the experimental group became more favourable towards computer education. There was correlation between age and attitude towards use of computer. There was significant difference in the pre and post scores of the experimental group on knowledge in CAI and attitude towards use of computer.

Mike Savage, Ed. and Prem Naidoo, Ed (2002): This book contains case studies concerning the popularization of science and technology education in Africa. Science and technology, and science and technology education, play an important role in the development of a country's economy, environment, social relations, and other sectors. African countries recognize this role and many have committed considerable resources to the development of science and technology and their educational systems. In African countries, science and technology education stresses the memorizing of facts rather than problem solving, and concentrates on the teaching and learning of a cultural and irrelevant science and technology. African countries must, therefore, recognize the need to promote, develop, and sustain a relevant science and technology culture, which includes problem solving and indigenous aspects, in order to narrow the gap between them and industrialized countries.

Pascal G. Zachary (2003): U.S. academics and business professionals can help make the information sector an engine for economic development in Africa. The steady flow of educated people out of Africa creates a brain drain, putting great pressure on university and technical professionals who remain behind, raising costs, and reducing output. U.S. universities, with the support of government and international organizations, can play an e-Learning and Application of Educational Technology in African Countries, or in Contexts Relevant to Africa important role in helping African universities and their surrounding technical communities. The growing computer community in Africa has the skills and interest to take advantage of stronger links to U.S. computer scientists and electrical engineers, who can make a few inexpensive and flexible efforts to integrate the African high-tech sector. The writer illustrates the drive to develop a home-grown cadre of software programmers and computer engineers in Africa with the case of several individuals from the growing computer community of Ghana.

Elizabeth A. White, Shelly B. Wepner and Donna C. Wetzel (2003): A study examined assistive technology initiatives in higher education. Data were obtained from public and private universities and colleges. Results highlighted the complexities of assistive technology's application in higher education and the lack of a specific plan in preservice education. Efforts by some institutions to integrate assistive technology in education courses and a national assistive technology initiative are discussed.

Shelley B. Wepner, Liging Tao and Nancy M. Ziomek (2003): The purpose of this study is to identify ways in which teacher educators shift responsibilities to infuse technology into their methodology courses and student teaching assignments, and to see if there are changes in students' skills as a result of new requirements. Three education faculty and 39 students participated. The following data sources were used: faculty's reflection journals; observations of student presentations in real classrooms and in college classrooms; students' reflection journals; students' evaluation of the technology requirements; and students' lesson plans. Pre- and post-study technological surveys showed significant differences in two areas. Four general categories of shifting responsibilities emerged from the study: (1) a shift in our role as instructor; (2) a shift in the way we plan for instruction and supervision; (3) a shift in our actual instruction and supervision; and (4) a shift in the way we monitor students' progress with technology infusion.

Bullock (2004): Moving from theory to practice: "An examination of the factors that perservice- teachers encounter as they attempt to gain experience teaching with technology during field placement experience."Found that teachers attitudes are major enabling and disabling factors in the adoption of technology.

Laura Czerniewicz. (2004): This article locates and describes the work of the Multimedia Education Group (MEG) at the University of Cape Town (UCT). This work is contextualised by three national and international challenges, these being (1) the need to increase access to new technologies and overcome the digital divide, (2) the need to respond to a new communication order, and (3) the urgency of transforming higher education in postapartheidSouth Africa. Operating in a fragmented policy environment, MEG has focused on developing educationally appropriate low-cost interventions, supporting academically disadvantaged students, andunderstanding the relationship between online and contact educational interventions. MEG's experiences e-Learning and Application of Educational Technology in African Countries, or in Contexts Relevant to Africa suggest that this kind of emergent work requires new ways of working, contributing to transformation within the institution itself. The work also creates epistemological challenges because it is interdisciplinary and because educational technology is a field that is not yet firmly established.

Minishi-Majanja and K. Mabel (2004): Information and communication technologies (ICTs) have become central in the education and training of Library and Information Science/Service (LIS) because of the great influence of these technologies on the profession. The purpose of this study was to determine the extent to which ICTs are applied in research, teaching, learning and academic administration, and establish the levels of ICT support available in South African LIS schools in terms of policies, infrastructure, hardware and human resource. The descriptive survey method was applied. Questionnaires were electronically mailed to 15 LIS education departments in January 2003, out of which 9 (60[percent]) responded. Some of the data was updated by respondents in July 2004. The findings indicated that all LIS departments in South Africa had responded to ICT developments by offering a wide range of ICT modules and embracing the use of ICTs in teaching, research and academic administration. It was observed that changes or modifications in existing qualifications and programmes are ongoing activities in several ins titutions. The majority of LIS departments in South Africa have interactive Web pages within the respective university/technikon Websites. However, for teaching and learning, only a few of the LIS schools used ICTs in presentation of lectures, while for research, teleconferencing and e-publishing ICTs were not yet extensively exploited. The study recommends that South African LIS schools should increase the use of ICTs in teaching and learning, as is the case in administration, to foster greater effectiveness. South African LIS schools should take advantage of experiences of online and distance education already well established among some universities in South Africa, in order to reach work-bound and other disadvantaged students due to distance from learning centres. The advantages of good Internet access should also be exploited and a mechanism for supporting accessibility should be lobbied for students from the technologically disadvantaged areas.

Paul Tiyambe and Zeleza Adebayo Olukoshi ed (2004): As the twenty-first century unfolds, African universities and indeed universities everywhere, are undergoing unprecedented change and confronting multiple challenges brought about by the vast and complex processes of globalisation and technological change. Powerful internal and external forces – political, pecuniary and paradigmatic – are reconfiguring all aspects of university life constituted around the triple mission of teaching, research and service. Important chapter: "Knowledge Creation and Dissemination in African Universities with Special Reference to Information and Communication Technologies (ICT):" e-Learning and Application of Educational Technology in African Countries, or in Contexts Relevant to Africa.

Philip M. Uys, Paul Nleya, and G.B. Molelu (2004): This paper analyses and suggests possible technological innovation strategies in higher educational institutions in Africa. The paper describes management issues in the implementation of eLearning with particular reference to its usage in higher education abroad and in Africa, and also suggests appropriate approaches for technological innovation of higher education in Africa. The major findings of the paper, which are based on three case studies, suggest that eLearning needs to be implemented within a strategically developed framework based on a clear and unified vision and a central educational rationale. The findings further highlight the importance of using a combination of strategies--top-down, bottom-up and inside-out--during the diffusion process to attain coherence, collegiality and ownership. The process of technological transformation is not a smooth translation process but one of dislocations, dilemmas and uncertainties and it is an art to effect change and sustainable technological transformation since people are central to this transformation process.

Michelle Selinger (2004): An eleven country internal evaluation of the Cisco Networking Academy program across Europe, the Middle East and Africa, revealed a number of issues related to the globalization of e-learning. The Academy program is a 280-hour web-based course that teaches students to install, maintain and troubleshoot computer networks. It was developed in the US by educators and Cisco network specialists and is taught in educational institutions in over 150 countries worldwide. Hitherto research on cultural influences on teaching and learning have been limited to overseas students being taught in an unfamiliar culture or online by teachers with unfamiliar pedagogical strategies. Through interviews with both students and teachers and observation in classrooms, this study reveals how important local tutors are in helping students adapt to the style of the material and to make a course developed in another country both culturally and pedagogically relevant.

Cheryl Brown and Laura Czerniewicz (2005): This paper examines the resources that students in five higher education institutions in South Africa have access to, in order to use ICTs for teaching and learning. The paper uses a complex conceptual framework of access to describe the kinds of access to specific resource groupings that students have available to them. The framework is summarized here. In particular, the paper explores whether and how different groups of students access specific resource groupings differently. Finally the paper touches briefly on the relationships between specific groups of students, their access to resource groupings, and their use of ICTs for teaching and learning. The need for this study arises from a transforming national and global environment where educational change is inextricably bound up with information and communication technologies (ICTs). At the same time, transformation imperatives, especially since the e-Learning and Application of Educational Technology in African Countries, or in Contexts Relevant to Africa South African 1994 elections, have required higher education institutions to foreground issues of social equity and redress. Thus technology and transformation, access and diversity are closely interwoven matters, which need to be simultaneously understood and acted on.

Jenny Leach (2005): This paper is addressed to the international community of educators and educational policy makers who, it is argued, need to commit to joint research and creative action in respect of the challenge of Education for All (EFA). The first section, A Global Challenge for Teacher Development, sets out: the implications for teacher education of the Education For All agenda; the potential of new information and communication technologies (ICT) in addressing this problem; an overview of an applied research project exploring new models of teacher education using ICT in rural and resource challenged environments. In the second section Towards New Models of Professional Development, four categories of teacher professional knowledge from this model are used to interpret and explore the findings of the project and its impact on teacher knowledge and development. The paper concludes that ICT can no longer be viewed as some sort of optional pedagogic strategy available in ever increasing sophistication, as well as quantity, to only a small proportion of the world's teachers. They need to be seen as an essential aspect of teaching's cultural toolkit in the 21st century, affording new and transformative models of development that extend the nature and reach of teacher learning wherever it takes place. Such models must be experienced, shared and evaluated by educators world wide if the global commitment to achievement of the EFA targets is to become a reality.

John M. Mativo (2005): A report on the challenges that face the Department of Technology at the University of Eastern Africa in Baraton, Kenya, is provided. Some of the challenges facing this department include its rural location, lack of trained and qualified personnel, inadequate facilities, and students' dependence on government employment.

Kirkup & Kirkwood, (2005); Wagner, (2001): who argue that it is the contextualized teaching and learning needs which ought to drive the ICT intervention, rather than the technology itself. In South Africa contextualisation of teaching and learning requires a tight walk between higher education imperatives and social-cultural context of the educational landscape. Although educational technology is not the panacea for educational challenges, it does leverage and extend traditional teaching and learning activities in certain circumstances and hence has the potential to impact on learning outcomes.

Maria Athaide (2005): "A Study of the Effectiveness of the Training Program conducted by Intel- India for Secondary School Teachers" To list suggestions for increasing the effectiveness of the Intel Training Program in terms of the Training given to the Secondary School Teachers and its application in the use of computers in their subject teaching. The variables under study, namely, level of satisfaction of the Secondary School Teachers towards the Intel's Training Program, Extent of Application of the Training Program, Types of Intel's Training Program, The categories of the schools under study, Teaching Experience of the Secondary School Teachers, Accessibility to computers, Accessibility to the Internet, Aid status of the schools, Special timetable, and Teacher's Commitment to the Professional use of computer technology have been well identified. The investigator has conducted ethnographic-cum-survey study.Interview, observation and questionnaires were the tools/techniques used for the study. The investigator has tried to observe the reliability of the ethnographic data through internal and external reliability techniques and triangulation, and internal, external and construct validity. The content validity and characteristics of the questionnaires were well established.

Susan McKenney (2005): This article describes research on the quality of a computer program designed to help secondary level science teachers in southern Africa create exemplary paper-based lesson materials. Results of this study show that the content, support, and interface of the program combine to form a tool that is considered by both users and experts to be valid and practical. Findings further indicate that it has the potential to help users create good quality materials while learning from the design process, but that this potential depends primarily on how the program is implemented.

Tim Unwin. (2005): There is a gulf between the rhetoric of those advocating the use of ICT in education in Africa and the reality of classroom practice. This paper explores some of the reasons for this, and outlines a possible framework for the successful implementation of teacher training programmes that make advantageous use of appropriate ICTs. It argues that six fundamental principles of good practice must be addressed for such programmes to be effective: a shift from an emphasis on 'education for ICT' to the use of 'ICT for education'; an integration of ICT practice within the whole curriculum; a need for integration between pre-service and in-service teacher training; a need for the development of relevant and locally produced content; a need for appropriate educational partnerships; and an emphasis on the development of sustainable costing models. The paper concludes with a framework for action to deliver the very real benefits of ICT for teacher training in Africa. Tools and Techniques : CAI programmes on 5 units for learning each language were used for conducting the experiment. Different tools for the study, namely, criterion tests and opinionnaires have been used.

Daniel G. Alemneh and Samantha K. Hastings. (2006): The synergies of numerous emerging trends are shaping creation, access, use and preservation of information resources. The digital library environment provides scholars with access to more diverse and previously unavailable contents that span myriad technologies across institutions and nations. Although the uses of Internet technologies provide new directions for scholarship, there are discrepancies among nations and regions. These technologies have not been fully exploited in Africa in particular. As research and scientific inquiry depend on both the availability of heterogeneous resources from multiple sources and their openness to easy and continued access, addressing the universal access issue is paramount. This article discusses and provides an overview of some of the barriers or principal factors most likely to influence Africa's efforts in harnessing the full power of the Internet and ICT for teaching and learning.

Margaret Wallace (2006): The article highlights the need for a strategic approach to e-Learning development with clear guidance information available to all. Electronic learning has the potential to transform the way teaching is both e-Learning and Application of Educational Technology in African Countries, or in Contexts Relevant to Africa designed and delivered. Government at local, national and international levels have heralded the advent of e-Learning as a positive contribution towards the achievement of a wider lifelong learning agenda. In actuality, the adoption of online learning practices by public education providers has been much slower than anticipated. Frustrated by limited progress to date, educational agencies have recently sought to identify major factors impinging development. Variables such as access to technology, adequate funding strategies and increased awareness of initiatives at senior level within educational institutions have all become the focus of further research. The issues of cultural change among academic communities and reengineering of operational procedures within schools, colleges and universities can be seen as the key determinants of successful widespread adoption and development of e-Learning practice. This article reports the findings of research carried out within the Scottish further education community. The primary research conducted investigated academics' copyright concerns as a barrier to the widespread adoption of e-Learning practice. The study surveyed Scottish further education academic staff regarding levels of usage of existing e-Learning environments and found copyright concerns to be the legal area of most concern, even greater than data protection or freedom of information. Copyright was the most frequent area of request for legal awareness training among teaching practitioners. The survey and report takes account of major initiatives in e-Learning development including JISC studies, funding council reports and governmental strategic planning. Detailed consideration of the impact of these initiatives form a major part of the secondary research along with an analysis of staff development support to date. A need for coherent training and guidance focused on practitioners' needs was highlighted by the research. Reflections were that this had not yet been made available in a form recognized by the practitioners. Following the adoption of the European Union Copyright Directive into British law in 2003, the exemptions afforded to education have been radically altered. The article also contains an in-depth analysis of these changes and a review of existing literature on the subject.

Obajemu. A.S,A. Ibegwam (2006): A survey of 84 participants at the Cataloguing, Classification and Indexing Group of the Nigeria Library Association workshop in 2004 was carried out with a view to determining the impact of the annual workshop on the application of information and communications technologies (ICT) to cataloguing and classification, in Nigerian libraries. The work covered 43 libraries-universities, polytechnics, colleges of education, research institutes and ministries/parastatals/agencies which cut across the 6 geopolitical zones of Nigeria (North-East, North-West, North-Central, South-West, South-East and South-South).- The data analysed showed that the workshops organised in recent years had spurred the action of the participants at those workshops to further pursue ICT (78[percent]). The findings also revealed that the workshops have had positive impact on the participants with respect to the application of ICT to cataloguing and classification. Recommendations for libraries that intend to computerise their catalogues were proffered.

Therese Laferriere, Mary Lamon and Carol K. K. Chan (2006): With the advent of the knowledge era, teacher education needs to prepare teachers to face the changing technological contexts and to model pedagogies and tools for better forms of learning. Despite much enthusiasm about the roles of technology in education, its role in transforming teacher learning, in ways aligned with advances in the learning sciences and contemporary socio-cultural perspectives, few changes have occurred. While many teacher educators are turning away from technology after early attempts met with mitigated success, some are pushing the boundaries of teacher education and professional activity systems. This paper identifies and analyzes emerging trends and models in elearning for teacher education and professional development from the developing research base; both international trends and current developments in the Asia-Pacific region are described. We focus on e-Learning and Application of Educational Technology in African ountries, or in Contexts Relevant to Africa progressively more sophisticated approaches including: (1) renewal of delivery of information with online repositories and courses; (2) rise of web-supported classrooms; (3) participation in learning networks and communities; and (4) knowledge creation in knowledge-building communities. We propose that technological innovations accompany social and pedagogical changes, and for the betterment of education, teachers need to play key roles as owners and designers of their learning. The potentials and challenges regarding these emerging trends in e-learning and their implications for teacher learning are examined.

Lunenberg, Korthagen and Swennen (2007) Howey and Zimpher, (1990); and Lanier and Little (1986): have found that there were very few studies that have examined the role of the teacher educator in the teaching learning processor of the graduate teacher in general and in the context of change in particular.They have concluded that "in order to improve the impact of teacher education, and especially the potential of teacher education to develop new visions of learning and the related practices in their graduates, one aspect that we have to look at carefully is the role of the teacher educator and the educational practices within teacher education itself".

Fui Tong Lee & and Boon Han Yeap (2009): "The Use of Educational Technologies in University Teaching & Learning" student to participate and engage in dialogues and discussions with lecturer and among themselves in their learning experience. Each of these teaching techniques has its own merit and their applicability in classroom environment depends on the learning/teaching situation such as subject content, availability of new multimedia technology, duration of lecture, level of student knowledge, interaction history of student/lecturer, level of Conclusions: The use of modern educational interactive learning tools and web-based technologies are indeed powerful resources that enhance and support quality learning and enrich the students' learning experience. The traditional T&L model is not relevant to real student needs due to today rapidly changing environment. Lectures should focus not only on the material content, in-class activities, or discussion but how to actively engage the students with the material in ways that promote student learning. This will involve a lecturer total commitment in teaching that take full responsibility by actively doing everything to cause the student to learn. The lecture content must be valuable, relevant, and interesting and related to realworld problems that enable students to make the necessary connections between theory and real life applications. The challenges for lecturers are to influence students in positive ways and simultaneously be able to flexibly adapt a wide range of learning situations and educational technologies evolved from time to time. To be effective, one must consciously attempt to be flexible, changing plans, actions or goals in response to the changing interests and needs of today students and/or from the many unplanned and unforeseen events that happen during the course of the lecture.

Kirsti Ala-Mutka (2009): "PROBLEMS IN LEARNING AND TEACHING PROGRAMMING"- a literature study for developing visualizations in the Codewitz-Minerva project, Institute of Software Systems, Learning to program is a complex task and teachers should design their teaching approachescarefully. The traditional approach of concepts first is common and found to be effective, althoughalso different approaches exist. There are plenty of typical novice programming errors, many of which are well collected into the technical report by Pane and Myers They present features and issues that should be taken into account when designing support systems for programming novices, and their work is useful also in connection to developing Codewitz materials.

Sevilay Sahin & Esen Turan (2009): "The effects and uses of educational technology in learning and teaching". In this study, the effect of technology on learning and teaching in a classroom environment is investigated. It is widely known that, the effect of technology in the classroom is highly productive. But to what extent and under what circumstances it should be applied depend on different factors such as; background knowledge of teachers about the teaching equipments they use, the ability to use this technology, the methods, strategies and techniques about using it, students' perceptions of technology, technological supports offered by the school, etc. As a result, technology is not an end itself, it should be supported by some other mean.

Shaheeda Jaffer Dick Ng'ambi Laura Czerniewicz (2009): "The role of ICTs in higher education in South Africa: one strategy for addressing teaching and learning challenges" Many choices for using Information and Communication Technologies (ICTs) in education are based on echnological possibilities rather than educationally needs. In developing countries where higher education is fraught with several challenges, there is increasing pressure to ensure that technological possibilities are viewed in the context of educational needs. This paper argues that in South Africa, a central role of educational technology is to provide additional strategies which can be used to address the serious academic challenges faced by educators and students in higher education. Higher education is faced with numerous challenges: general, educational and specifically to do with teaching and learning. The latter challenges include lack of academic preparedness, multilingual needs in first language settings, large classes and inadequate curriculum design. Using case studies from one higher educational institution, this paper shows how specific and carefully considered interventions using ICTs can be used to address these teaching and learning concerns. This paper demonstrates by means of examples of curriculum projects at one higher education institution how educational needs shape educational technology enhanced curriculum interventions. The paper concludes that educational technology interventions should be based on educational needs as opposed to technological concerns.

2.1.3 Indian Studies Related To Learners

Manoharan. M (1988): Studied the relative effectiveness of print media. The main objective of this study was to find out experimentally the relative effectiveness of the print media in terms of knowledge gain and retention of knowledge. Experimental method was used for this study. Traditional media were found to have a slight edge over new media in terms of influencing knowledge gain.

Rajamony. N, (Nov, 1989): "conducted a study on 'Recent development in educational technology." Educational technology via the systems approach should be flexible enough to react to new knowledge about the process of human learning, and also to new developments in teaching/learning approaches and methods (Percival and Elligton, 1986). Etton (1977) identified three broad lines mass communication, individualized learning and group learning, along which educational technology area was evolved through successive phases of research, development and use since 1945. In the research phase, the related basic concepts and techniques were developed which were converted into practical teaching and learning techniques together with their associated support materials the development phase that followed, leading to their widespread used.

Solachi, T (1991): Conducted a study on availability and utilization of Educational Technology in the Higher Secondary Schools of districts in Tamil Nadu. The Study revealed that the utilization rate was higher in urban schools as compare to rural schools. Government and aided schools are also differed in their utilization rate. The aided schools did a better job between boys and girls schools, the boys schools utilized educational technology more. Science teachers are compared to humanities teachers utilized more non-projected and projected visual aids. They also use more community resource technology. Students were found to have well understood Simple Tense, Continuous Tense, Perfect Tense, Simple Modal Auxiliaries, Perfect Modal Auxiliaries, Infinitive,Participle, Causal Construction and Imperative Sentence through self learningmaterial as evident through the pre-test and post-test status through meanachievement on respective sub-criterion tests. Students were found to have well understood Active and Passive Voice throughself learning material. For both the schools of rural and urban areas, Learning through Self-Learning Material and Traditional Teaching was found almost equal on Simple Tense,Continuous Tense, Perfect Tense, Simple Modal Auxiliaries, Perfect Modal Auxiliaries and participle, as no significant difference has been reported on the mean gain scores. No significant difference was found in the mean scores on Learning on Infinitive through Self Learning Material in urban areas , whereas, it was found significant in rural areas. No significant difference was found in the mean scores on Learning on causal construction through Self Learning Material in rural areas , whereas, it was found significant in urban areas. Learning on Active and Passive Voice through Self Learning Material has been reported significantly greater in urban as well as rural areas as compared to that of control groups. There has been found a significant difference among the mean gain scores of students on Simple Tense taught through Self Learning Material in all the four selected schools. Similar has been found the status on Continuous Tense and Perfect Tense. No significant differences have been found among the mean gain scores of students on Simple Modal Auxiliaries, Perfect Modal Auxiliaries, Infinitive, Participle, Causal Construction and Imperative Sentence. No significant differences have found among the mean gain scores of students on Active and Passive Voice taught through Self Learning Materials in all the four schools. Students of the two selected schools have been found to gain significantly greater on Active and Passive

Voice as evident through the retention test. The Hypothesis that " There is no significant influence of gender, level of IQ and their interaction on achievement in Active and Passive Voice of the students learnt through Self-Learning Materials by considering pre-achievement in Active and Passive Voice as covariate" has been rejected at .05 level. The Self-Learning Material has been found to have greater impact on the students of General Stream than that of the Science Stream. The Self-Learning Material has been found to have greater impact on the students of urban area than that of the rural area. The Hypothesis that " There is no significant influence of level of IQ, stream and their interaction on achievement in Active and Passive Voice of the students learnt through Self-Learning Materials by considering pre-achievement in Active and Passive Voice as covariate" has been rejected at .05 level. The Hypothesis that " There is no significant influence of level of IQ, stream and their interaction on achievement in Active and Passive Voice of the students learnt through Self-Learning Materials by considering pre-achievement in Active and Passive Voice as covariate" has been rejected at .05 level. The Hypothesis that " There is no significant influence of level of IQ, area and their interaction on achievement in Active and Passive Voice of the students learnt through Self-Learning Materials by considering pre-achievement in Active and Passive Voice as covariate" has been rejected at .05 level. The self- learning material has been found to have better impact on the students of General Stream than that of the Science Stream. It has been found to have better impact on the students of urban area than that of the rural area. Gender, level of IQ and the interaction between the gender and level of IQ have been found to have no significant effect on the mean achievement of the students on Active and Passive Voice learnt through Self-Learning Materials. The self-learning material has been found to have a better impact on boys than girls. It has been found to have a better impact on the students of general stream than that of science stream. There has been found a significant interaction effect of the gender and stream on the mean scores on main criterion test at post-test stages. The self-learning material has been found to have a better impact on the students of urban area than that of the rural area. The self-learning material has been found to have a better impact on the students of average level than that of higher level. There has been found a significant effect of the interaction of level of IQ and area on the mean scores on main criterion test at post-test stages. There has been found a significant effect of the interaction of stream and area on the mean scores on main criterion test at post-test stages. The students have been found to have favourable opinion on the self-learning material

Interactive Educational Systems Design. (1995): Report on the effectiveness of technology in schools. This report provides software developers and publishers with research that will enable them to improve educational technology so that it continues to have a significant positive impact on student achievement, self-concept and attitudes, and on the interactions in the learning environment for students of all ages, capabilities, socio-economic backgrounds, and areas of interest.

Pullias, D. (1997): Modular laboratories provide technology education students with valuable experiences, but they are not the total solution. Technology education can aid problem solving, technological literacy, and school-wide curriculum integration, but not within the limits of the modular environment.

Anshuman Das (1998): "Exploring effectiveness of computer assisted learning material on Rhymes in different modes"Sample: Seven rhymes were presented in 5 different modes, namely, T, GT, TM, GTM, andGTMR to 5 different groups of students, respectively, drawn from a total of 169 studentsof Second Standard of Baroda High School, Baggi Khana (1996-97) on the basis ofsystematic random sampling. Each group comprised of 20 students.Findings of the Study are, Composite modes of presentation may not ensure higher cognitive language learning. Intelligibility of a message is a function of sender, message, medium,mode, receiver, and the environment.

Thatte C.H., (1998): University of Mumbai, Mumbai: "An Experimental Study of the Relative Effectiveness of Programmed Learning and Learning Through Audio Visual Aids with reference to certain selected topics from the syllabus of Science for Std. V to VII in Greater Bombay"Sample:Eight Schools of Greater Mumbai were selected in all. Twenty four different classes were considered and the total number of students was 1381. Findings are1. AV aids method was found to be significantly more effective than the Programmed Learning Method and the Traditional method in terms of achievement at Std. V, VI, and VII.2. Programmed Instruction Method was found to be significantly more effective than the Traditional Method in terms of achievement at Std. V, VI, and VII. 3. Programmed Learning Method and Audio Visual Method are more successful when the classes are small , at the same time they are more effective for average students.4. Male students and female students, both, equally benefited through the AVmethod as well as Programmed Learning Method. No significant effect ofinteraction between treatment and sex was found on the achievement of students.

Anjali Khirwadkar (1999): "Developing a computer software for learning Chemistry at Standard IX"Sample:One of the English medium schools of Baroda City was taken for implementing the developed software. One section of Standard XI Science was taken and thirty students were selected randomly as sample for the experimental group and rest of the students of the section constituted the control group.Findings are, The developed software package was found to be effective in terms of academicachievement of the students. The students and teachers were found to have favourable opinion towards the software package. There was found an interaction effect of IQ, motivation and opinion of students on their academic achievement.

Kadhiravan. S (1999): Conducted a study on "Effectiveness of computer Assisted Instruction in relation to students use. Among the instructional strategies, viz. LM, CAI and CAIPI, CAIPI was the most effective instructional objectives in physics at higher secondary stage. Among the three instructional strategies, CAIPI is the most effective one in terms of its effectiveness in realizing the instrumental objectives in the context of contents with below difficulty level. There was a significant difference among different instructional strategies, viz. LM, CAL and CAIPI in enhancing the students use of SRL strategies. CAI and CAIPI had some influence on students use of SRL strategies while lecture method had not. There was significant difference among the instructional strategies, viz. LM, CAI and CAIPI in terms of their effectiveness in enhancing the retention of what was already learn in physics. There was a different effect on the cognitive development of the students in physics due to their use of self-regulated learning strategies. The study cites 193 references.

Yashobanta Samal (2000): Ut kal University, Bhubaneshwar: "Effectiveness of the School Broadcast Programmes of All India Radio (AIR) and Educational Television (ETV) Programme s of Doordarshan with reference to school achievement of the learners"Sample:A sample of 120 students and 20 teachers has been used for the study. Also, 20 ETV Programmes and 10 Educational Radio Programmes were selected for the study. Six tasks were constructed for the study.Findings:1. Both the ETV and School Broadcast programmes have been found to havepositive effect on school achievement of pupils. 2. There have been found mixed reactions of students and teachers regardingcontents and presentation of the ETV and School Broadcast Programmes.3. It is really a matter of concern that none of the schools was found utilizing the ETV and School Broadcast Programmes in an institutionalized manner.

Jyoti Tare (2001): Rani Durgavati University, Jabalpur: "A Study of the Effectiveness of Branching Variety of Programmed Instructional Material as Diagnostic and Remedial Tool in Chemistry for Secondary Classes in Jabalpur Division"Sample: 280 students were selected from different Government Higher Secondary Schools of urban and rural areas of Jabalpur Division.Findings:1. The achievement of the experimental group was found significantly greater than the achievement of the control group. 2. The achievement of the urban girls through PLM was found significantly higher than that of the urban boys. 3. No significant difference was found in the achievement of boys and girls of rural areas in the post-test on atomic structure and chemical bonding. 4. 135 boys out of 180 and 64 girls out of 99 wanted to continue the study with the PLM on both the topics. 5. The weakness of individual students were diagnosed and removed when branched frames on both the topics were administered.

Kumar. K.L. (2002): Part of a special section on e-learning prospective in the Asia-Pacific region. The writer discusses the need for e-learning in the African context. He reviews some of the limited studies of the use of e-learning in Africa and the progress made in this area South East Asia. The writer concludes that innovative measures must be adopted to teach electronic courses in science and technology, where practical work is crucial to both the understanding of the concepts and the growth of the individual to the profession.

Nishi Jain (2002): "A Study of IGNOU Teleconferencing for Distance Learners"Findings: Very few participants were found attending the teleconferencing programmes. Usually the participants were found attending the programmes attentively. Participants wanting to ask questions seemed more interested in the programmes. It was found that the time allotted for the talkback session usually was not enough. Some learners having vernacular background expressed apprehension about the comprehensibility of the programmes. They felt inhibitions in discussing and asking questions. There were mixed responses regarding the effectiveness of the teleconferencing programmes. Some found these programmes very exciting and wonderful, whereas others could not utilize these programmes properly. Proper coordination is required among all the personnel involved in IGNOU Teleconferencing.

Monica Landoni and Paloma Diaz (2003): This paper addresses the need for a conceptual approach to researching, e-learning instructional design and the technologies employed as a basis for e-learning. It describes the goals of this issue of the Journal of Digital Information. Design and usability of e-learning objects are the main focus of the papers in this issue. It provides readers with some insights into the state-of-the-art of research in usability in eeducation, showing how independent this area has become. There are still a number of open challenges, such as the holy grail of setting recognised and workable standards, and the definition of criteria for measuring how successful e-learning objects are in achieving their objectives. This is what makes research in this area such a challenge.

Satoru Fujitani, Bhattacharya, Madhumita and Kanji Akahori (2003): Part of a special issue on online learning and information technology in the Asia-Pacific region. The implementation of information and communications technology (ICT) in education and online learning in Japan is discussed. Although there have been ambitious research and development efforts, the use of ICT and online learning has not been particularly appreciated at large numbers of schools in Japan. However, a project called E-Japan Strategies is now underway to emphasize the educational use of ICT and progress in the implementation of ICT in schools. Moreover, a new curriculum that puts emphasis on the use of ICT will have powerful inducements to educate students with a certain level of knowledge and skills. A suggested model for online learning in education is discussed.

Chantahiem Chamnan (2004): "A Study of Availability And Utilization of Educational Media in Secondary Schools of Thailand"Sample for the StudyMultistage random sampling technique was used for drawing the samples of 576 students, 620 teachers, 75 media-in-charge and 75 administrators.Tools Used:Checklists and Questionnaires were used for the study.Findings of the Study: A majority of the respondents have accepted the suitability of the available media in the schools. Majority of the teachers have showed their satisfaction in the use of educational media. 50% of the sample schools were found to have physical problems, mostly related with physical facilities of the classroom and laboratory.Such schools were not having sufficient and workable equipments, software, and infrastructure. The modern media were found to face more of problems as compared to traditional media in terms of skilled human resource. The problems related to administrative system were mostly related with the non- cooperative behaviour or due to less insight of the administrators. The problems related to supporting staff were mostly related with the proper full time appointment of the technical person. The educational media were found largely under used. The power point, CAI, and CMI were never used in their schools as responded by about 20% of the teacher sample. Suitability of available software related to Thai and English languages was perceived less as compared to other subjects. Availability of high tech media was greater in big size schools as compared to the medium and small size schools.

Suwanna Ruttanathummatee (2004): "Effectiveness of Computer Assisted Instruction for Primary School Students: AnExperimental Study". Taking this into consideration, the government of Andhra Pradesh supplied 10,000 television sets and video cassette players to selected M.P.P. Schools in the state. A colour television and radio cum cassette player were supplied to some of the school. Many head masters and teachers expressed their difficulties in making use of audio visual aids supplied. To find the difficulties faced by them in the effective use of aids, this study was taken up.Primary teachers are very poor in the operation of hardware. Hence, it is recommended that the primary teachers be given training in hardware.

Darshana Chaudhari, (2005): "Techno-pedagogic analysis of children ETV programmes and their effectiveness in terms of achievement with and without discussion and perception of students and teachers". post-test, experimental and control group design was employed for the study. 60 students of Std.V of Shree Krishna Hindi medium school constituted the sample for the study. Also all the 5 teachers teaching Std.V were selected . 5 programmes were selected purposively out of the 15 recorded. Techno-pedagogic analysis tool, achievement test on each selected CETV Program, reaction scale, and un-structured interview were employed. Content analysis , presentation analysis, independent 't' test and % analysis were used for the study. The programmes were largely found effective techno-pedagogically in terms of mediagenicity, audio-visual compatibility, contiguity between text and animation and between audio and visuals, media language proficiency, use of technological aids, corresponsdence among communication elements, and view composition. All the six programmes were at knowledge level, 5 at understanding level, whereas 4 were at application level. Most of the programmes focused on receiving and responding. Three focused on valuing also. One of the 6 programmes focused on imitation ,manipulation and articulation level. There was significant difference between the mean gain scores of control and experimental group in all the 6 programmes. In 5 out of six programmes , the mean achievement of the group with discussion was found significantly higher than that of without discussion . Children and teachers were found to have positive views regarding the programs.

Jaykumar Rathod (2005): "Development and Implementation of an Information Technology Based Instructional Package for English Grammar to Gujarati medium students of Standard VIII of Jamnagar City" post-test control group design was employed for the study. The development of the IT based instructional package was done through Microsoft power point. 100 students were randomly selected from standard VIII of Smt. G.S. Mehta Municipal Girls High School, Jamnagar. These students were further divided into Experimental and Control groups. Two parallel tests were constructed by the investigator to study the achievement of the students. These two tests were constructed on the content topics simple present tense, present continuous tense, preposition- in, on, under and behind and possessive forms of has and have. Also, a five point reaction scale was constructed to study the reactions of the students on the developed package. Mean, SD, uncorrelated 't' value and chi square were computed for data analysis. The developed IT based instructional package was found to be effective for teaching English Grammar because there was found a significant difference in the gain mean scores of the experimental group and control group. The students were found having positive reactions towards the developed IT based instructional package.

Rakesh Pardeshi (2005): "A study of the relative effectiveness of CAI and CAIPI in learning Trigonometry by English medium students of Standard IX of Baroda City"The study was conducted in the three sections of Standard IX of Zenith High School, Baroda, dividing each section into two groups- experimental and control. The CAI was developed using Flash-MX, Directors and Corel Draw 11.0 along with the Internet. An achievement test was constructed for administering as pre-test and post-test. The data were analyzed through mean, SD, uncorrelated 't' and ANOVA. No significant difference has been found in the mean achievement scores of the groups in mono, diad and triad. No significant difference has been found in the mean achievement scores of the experimental group in mono, diad , triad and control groups, respectively. Significant difference has been found in the mean achievement scores of the experimental group in triad and control group. The students were found to have positive reactions towards the developed CAI.

Gautam, A. Panchal, N. (2006): "Development and Tryout of Self-Learning Materials in English subject on the unit of 'Active and Passive Voice' for the Students of Standard-XII"Sample:A sample of 192 students has been drawn using compatible sampling techniques. Two pre-experimental groups were constituted, each having 32 students, one from Rural Area, whereas, the other one from Urban area, wherein, the sample units were duly distributed as Science Stream and General Stream, Boys and Girls. Similarly, one experimental group and one control group were constituted from urban area, whereas, another set of experimental and control groups was constituted from rural area, each having 32 students, distributed fairly stream-wise and gender-wise. Tools and techniques: Desai Verbal and Non-Verbal Group Intelligence Test, and the Sub-Criterion Tests, Main Criterion Test, and Opinionnaire constructed by the investigator were used for the Study. The characteristics of all the tools used for the study were well established. The data have been gathered systematically.

The Influence of System Characteristics on e-learning use (2006): The benefits of an e-learning system will not be maximized unless learners use the system. This study proposed and tested alternative models that seek to explain student intention to use an e-learning system when the system is used as a supplementary learning tool within a traditional class or a stand-alone distance education method. The models integrated determinants from the well-established technology acceptance model as well as system and participant characteristics cited in the research literature. Following a demonstration and use phase of the e-learning system, data were collected from 259 college students. Structural equation modeling provided better support for a model that hypothesized stronger effects of system characteristics on e-learning system use. Implications for both researchers and practitioners are discussed.

Sahaya Mary, R. & I. Paul Raj (2008): "Scientific Attitude of Upper Primary students towards science learning". The investigator used the Scientific Attitude Opinionnaire as a tool.From the above analysis. The investigator found that the facors domicile, gender, locality of the school, medium of instruction and size of the family do not influence their scientific attitude and achievement in science. But the age and religion of the students influence their scientific attitude and the achievement in science. It shows the age and religion influence the upper primary students attitude towards science learning.

Ishad Hussain & Muhammad Aslam (2009): "Role of mobile technology in promoting campus-wide learning environment" The present study examines the role of mobile technology in promoting campus-wide learning environment.The population of the study consisted of all the Ph.D scholars (N= 83) and faculty (N=10) of the Department ofEducation, International Islamic University, Islamabad. The samples of the study comprised of 100% of boththe populations. The study was descriptive in nature, therefore survey approach was considered appropriate.The researchers used questionnaires as research tools developed on five point rating (likert) scale to collect thedata from the respondents (students and faculty respectively). The researchers personally administered thefinalized research tools (through pilot testing) to the respondents to collect the data.

The data collected was analyzed through applying the mean score and percentage and main findings were (i) 92% of the espondents (students and faculty) were of the opinion that mobile technology is appropriate for effective communication and interaction (ii). 94% of the respondents ((students and faculty) were of the view that mobile technology promotes flexible interactive learning environment (iii). 93% of the respondents (students) supported that they do face problems with technology. Keeping in view these findings, it was concluded that mobile technology is appropriate for research and education throughout the campus as it promotes effective interaction among faculty and scholars.

Kanmani. M. & Annaraja. P. (2009): "Influence of self-esteem and awareness of ICT on Academic Achievement of M.Ed. students."The sample consisted of randomly selected 42 M.Ed students. self-esteem and awareness of Information and communication Technology tools were used to gather data. Multiple correlation, Pearson Product mo0ment correlation co-efficient, t-test and F-test were used to analyze the data. The result clearly shows that there is a significant difference between the government-aided and university department M.Ed students, academic achievement; there is no correlation between self-esteem and awareness on information and communication technology, and there is no influence of self-esteem and awareness of information and communiction technology on academic achievement.

2.1.4 Foreign Studies Related to Teachers

Shade, D.D. (Ed.). (1992): Provides an overview of studies for possible application to instruction with children and computers and a starting point for in-depth research by listing bibliographic citations and author abstracts of nine selected studies in computer education.

Chidambaram, (1996): conducted a study on "Technical Knowledge of teachers in using audio-visual equipment in Mandal Praja Parishad School in Andhra Pradesh.Suggested to make the learning process, realistic and vivid, a rich galaxy of audio- visual aids can be used in the classroom. A variety of aids like pictures, maps, films, filmstrips, models, charts, graphs, etc., can be used. Audio-visual aids will supplement the spoken word. It will make the subject real, vivid, vital, interesting, and life-like. It develops concepts, improves attitudes and extends appreciation. It helps making learning permanent. Lastly, it will supplement the material in the text book.

Nirmal Sabharwal (Aug 1996): Conducted study on "Innovations in Teaching Technology". She found that such initiatives need to be disseminated and shared with others through an appropriate system that recognizes excellence and achievement and rewards performance. Thus further need to be applied replicated in the field. Such an effort would also reduce the gap between research and summer of research teachers and improve educational substantially.

Kumar. N (1998): Studies the prospects and problems in the use of Educational Media. The study attempted the explore the problem experienced by the teachers in using media in their classroom teaching in context of Agriculture Universities in India. The researcher found that most of the teachers are highly aware of different instructional media but only a few felt that they had media operating capability and media-production capability. Majority teachers are using only chalkboard as a teaching aid. Charts and posters are other media used by about 79% of teachers but only in some classes overall the level of media utilization by teachers is very poor.

Northwest Regional Educational Laboratory. (1998): Looks inside classrooms around the Northwest where teachers are using technology skillfully to teach subjects. Offers a guide to getting started, practical tips for using the Internet and selecting software.

Munther Mohammed Zyoud (1999): "Development of Computer Assisted English Language Teaching for VIII Standard Students. "Findings:The study reveals that when the computer is used to its full potential, it can help the students achieve more in learning vocabulary, grammar and comprehension to the learners with different IQ, motivation and attitude. It helps the students learn better because it provides them with a lot of freedom and responsibility to learn at their own pace. The students were found to have +ve attitude towards Computer Assisted EnglishLanguage instruction.

Usha Rani. P, (1999-2000): conducted a study on "Role of educational technology in teaching – learning of English language in higher education". She found that English language, the gift of the Britishers has come to stay in India as a second language. It is taught in schools and colleges as a vehicle of communication. The technology currently used is the lecture (face to face instruction) along with printed materials. Some teachers adopt different methods of interaction, keeping in view the age, interest, aptitudes and attitudes of the learners.

Usha Sri. V, (1999-2000): conducted a study of the use of technology by teachers. Teaching as a dynamic process has given a prime of place at technology. Technology lends the arts and science to teaching teacher's knowledge and effective use of technical devices, pave the way to effective teaching. It is the right technique that strengthens the capabilities of an ordinary teacher to become an effective teacher. Technical skills are many which lay emphasis on teacher's power of conceptualizing by hypothesizing and synthesizing. The more recent concept of teaching is a popular means of teacher of teaching competencies innovative techniques employed that actual sample of teaching indicate teacher's effectiveness considering the foregoing aspects, it is felt that the debate need not be on technology vs teacher but, technology for teachers how? Unless this clarification is arrived at technology remains unused, misused and abused by the teacher.

Shanti, S. (2001-2002): conducted a study of technologies of teaching in schools". She found that the traditional system of education the teacher was the pivot and the students had only anoninal role in the process of learning. Pupils remained passive and silent spectators. They were taught through the verbal method only their rote memory was tested by education. This scenario under went great changes after nineteenth century. The role of the teacher in the modern system of education has been influenced by philosophical, psychological, social, educational and technological factors. Many audio-visual aids were advocated for use in the teaching-leaning process. The electronic media is computer which has powerful application in instruction. Multimedia computer has come with the facilities of sound, animation, video interactions etc. It helps the students in learning the concepts without difficulties. Internet is now helpfull in sharing the information, not only with in the country but also between the countries. Creativity mindness appreciation and adventouress of out look In the existing curriculum of social studies. The contact matter did not focus on the variety and change in human behaviour in ground interaction with physical environment and social environment, development of cross cultural and international understanding and lastly successfully integration of the subject. It was not related to significant problems of today like industrial changes, population changes, pollution and urbanization. It did not provide for a spirit of inquiry flexibility, interaction between man and his environment, careful planning and experimentation.

Bhattacharya, M. (2002) : A special section on e-learning prospective in the Asia-Pacific region is provided. Articles discuss the differences between communities of practices and quasi-communities; the convergences of distance education, on-campus learning, and e-learning in Australia; a framework for the implementation of situated online, collaborative, problem-based activity; the emerging trend of knowledge management through e-learning in Indian higher education; adaptivity through the use of mobile agents in Web-based student modeling; and science and technology courses via e-learning in Africa.

Sneha M. Joshi, K. Pushpanadham, and Anjali Khirwadkar (2002): Part of a special section on e-learning prospective in the Asia-Pacific region. The Indian higher education system must integrate information and communication technologies (ICT) into the system for both academic and administrative tasks. As information is actively digitized, it is evident that both students and teachers of higher education will need access to and an ability to use ICT. The integration of ICT into higher education is not a simple task, and it will require large investments in hardware, software, e-Learning and Application of Educational Technology in African Countries, or in Contexts Relevant to Africa training, and content development. As the Indian government will not be able to provide the funds for such large investments, higher education must develop a close collaboration with private organizations, such as NIIT, Aptech, Microsoft, and Infosys.

Kante. C and Savani. V (2003): Countries across the globe are at different stages of integrating information and communications technologies (ICTs) into everyday practice, including teaching and learning. While the debate over the true value-added of e-learning versus face-to-face delivery of training content still rages, we all seem to agree that there is a tremendous opportunity for technology to revolutionize learning, just as it did for business. In this article, we will not attempt to compare e-learning with other content delivery mechanisms. Rather, we will focus our discussion on the educational potential of e-learning, with a particular emphasis on the seemingly endless opportunities associated with the use of e-learning in the developing world. We will elaborate on what we believe are the caveats for any e-learning initiative to attain its expected objectives, and convey the possibilities for application of e-learning in the difficult context of the developing world.

Vasanthi. A, and Hema, S. (2003): conducted a study on effectiveness of teaching chemistry for I year B.E. students through CAI. They found that there is significant difference between the mean gain score of the control group taught through TTM and the experimental group administered by the CAI in all units put together. There is no significant difference between the mean scores of pretest of control group taught through TTM and experimental group administered by CAI in all units put together (Electro chemistry Bonding). There is significant difference between the mean scores of post-test of control group taught through TTM and experimental group administered by CAI in all units put together. The study cites 15 references.

Beena Y. Desai (2004): "A Comparative Study of the Efficacy of Teaching Through the Traditional Method and the Multimedia Approach in the Subject of Home Science"Sample of the Study: The sample of the study is constituted of 98 students of B.A. first year home science (2001-2002) of Smt. J.P. Shroff Arts College, Valsad.Findings of the Study:The mean achievement of the experimental group was found significantly higher than that of the control group. From post-test to retention test almost equal reduction in performance was found in both the groups. The study has arrived at significant findings when caste, location, income, Std. XII examination marks, and IQ of the students wereconsidered as co-variables. The students were found to have favourable opinions towards the multimedia approach. The study has found the relative efficacy of teaching through the traditional method and the multimedia approach in the subject of Home Science, particularly, Proteins.

Yadav Kusum(2004) CASE, MSU, Baroda: "Development of an IT enabled Instructional Package for Teaching English medium students of Vadodara city". A single group pre-testand post-test design was employed for the study. 20 students were randomly selectedfrom Std. VIII of the New Era Senior Secondary School, Baroda. Pre-test, post-test andopinionnaire were used for the study. The data were analysed through 't' test, % scoresand content analysis. There was found a significant gain in terms of students'achievement through IT- enabled instructional package. It helped the students to learnkinds of sentences, namely, interrogative, assertive: affirmative, negative, imperative:orders or commands, and exclamatory. The students and teachers were found to havefavourable opinion towards the developed instructional package.

Hiralkumar M.Barot (2005): "A study of the effectiveness of CAI in Sanskrit for std. VIII students"The study was conducted to develop CAI in Sanskrit for Std. VIII students and to study its effectiveness in terms of mean achievement of students in Sanskrit and to study the reactions of the standard VIII students regarding the effectiveness of the developed CAI package. 86 students of Std. VIII of Shree Ambe Vidyalaya, Waghodia Road, Baroda constituted the sample for the study. A single group pre-test and post-test design was employed for the study .Achievement test and reaction scale were constructed by theinvestigator . Flash MX, Corel Draw 11 and Front Page were used for the development of software. 't' value, frequencies and % responses were used for data analysis . The developed CAI in Sanskrit was found effective in teaching Sanskrit to VIII std. students. The reactions of the students towards the developed CAI in Sanskrit were found positive.

Irfan Shah (2005): "ICT awareness, use and need of secondary and higher secondary teachers of English Medium Schools of Vadodara city" . A scale was constructed to collect the data regarding ICT awareness, use and need of a teacher with respect to different components of ICT, like, computer,Internet, OHP, LCD Projector, Radio, TV. 12 secondary and 10 higher secondary schools were selected using stratified random sampling technique. Further 60 secondary and 50 higher secondary teachers were selected @ 5 teachers from each selected school. A total of 90 teachers out of 110 responded. Data were analyzed using frequency, percentage, mean, SD, SE of mean, 't' value and ANOVA wherever necessary. There was found a low degree of ICT awareness, use and need of secondary and higher secondary teachers. The variables related to ICT awareness of teachers were teaching experience, age and total salary. The variables related with the ICT use of teachers were total salary and computer training. The variable related with the ICT need of teachers was the Degree Program which they attended at the University level.

In expanding the learning environment to include data bases, computer networks and other library resources through out the world, the internet makes it possible for students to shape their own education. Once the easy accessing protocols are learned, the student can drive into the resources in his or her home and library without the constant supervision and intervention of the teacher. Lao Tzulls dictum, "He who teacher least teacher better", describes students centered teaching learning and assessment environment, in which the students can access information from multiple perspective and learn to use this information to solve complete problems (Maskin, 1996).

Anil Tanaji Patil (2006): "Development of Multimedia Instructional System on Computer Education for B.Ed. Pupil Teachers".The Research Procedure designed by the investigator for the study is logical. After ascertaining the needs in the context of the Computer Education, the Multimedia Instructional System was well designed and developed. Authoring software Macromedia Director 7 seems to be quite compatible for the purpose. Alpha testing was done to further develop the system through the expertise available. The pilot testing of the prototype was done through two group pre-test post-test design (20(12+8), & 20(12+8)). Final implementation of the Multimedia Instructional Systemwas done on a sample of 64 pupil-teachers (32(20+12),32(20+12)), employing Solomon four group Experimental design.The Study has arrived at quite meaningful findings as follows:1.The present setting of teaching of computer education in B.Ed. Colleges was found unsatisfactory. 2. It was found feasible to design, develop and implement a computer based Multimedia Instruction System for the Computer Education. 3. No significant difference was found between the performance of the pupilteachers of control and experimental group on pre-test. 4. Significant difference was found between the performance of the pupil teachers of control group and experimental group on post-test. 5. Significant difference was found between the performance of the pupil teachers of control group from pre-test to post-test. 6. There is significant difference between the performance of the pupil- teachers of experimental group from pre-test to post-test. 7. There is significant difference between the gains in achievement in terms of scores in pre-test and post-test of the pupil- teachers from pre to post test. 8. There is significant difference between the performance of the pupil-teachers from control and experimental groups in retention test. It is an interesting and appealing Study, which has very evidently demonstrated its utility.

Sheela. G. (2006): conducted a study on "knowledge of information and communication technology and attitude towards teaching ICT among teacher educators". She found that teacher educators possessing good and poor knowledge of ICT differ in their attitude towards teaching ICT: Teacher educators with good knowledge of ICT have more favourable attitude towards teaching ICT. Male and female teacher educators do not differ significantly in their attitude towards teaching ICT. Teacher educators from private aided and private unaided colleges differ significantly in their attitude towards teaching ICT:Teacher educators from private unaided colleges were found to have more favourable attitude towards teaching ICT. A significant difference and found in the attitude of high experienced and less experienced teacher educators towards teaching ICT: teacher educators with less experience had a more favourable attitude towards teaching ICT than teacher educators with more experience. No significant difference was found in the attitude scores of teacher educators of arts and science streams towards teaching ICT. Teacher educators from rural and urban areas did not differ significantly in their attitude towards teaching of ICT.

Ramakrishna, A. (2008): " Teaching Aptitude of students of B.Ed Colleges." The reasearcher adopted a normative survey method to study the teaching aptitude and find its relation with EdCET ranks. The data revealed that the Mean for female group is more han that of the male group. There is a positive relationship between teaching aptitude and EdCET ranks of students.

Sumangala, V & Ushadevi, V.K. (2009): "Role Conflict, Attitude towards teaching profession and job satisfaction as predictors of success in teaching". The survey was carried out among 300 secondary school women teachers working in 53 government and private-aided secondary schools of ten districts of kerala.The tools used for the collection of data were Role conflict scale, job satisfaction inventory for teachers, scale of attitude towards teaching profession are capable of predicting success in teaching where as job satisfaction is not capable of predicting success in teaching. Role conflict has greater predictive efficiency when compared to attitude towards teaching profession which has the predictive efficiency.Thus 40.01 percent of the variance in success in teaching among the secondary school women teachers is accounted for by the variation due to role conflict and attitude towards teaching profession.

Mala Sharma, Sumar Sharma (2009): A study on " Attitude of science teachers towards project method" the main findings are: therre is no significant differe3nce in the attitude of male and female science teachers towards project method of teaching science. There is no significant difference in the attitude of science teachers having experience below 10 years and 10-20 years towards project method.

Reeta Chopra & Radhakanta Gartia (2009): "Accountablity of secondary school teachers in relation to their occupationasl stress". The investigator collected data from 120 secondary school teachers belonging to both private and government secondary schools. The investigators found the relationship of teachers accountability with occupational stress. Occupational stress was found to have a negative impact on accountablity of secondary school teachers. Furthermore, teachers who are highly occupationally stressed are less accountable. On the contrary teachers who are less occupationally stressed are more accountable towards their job. In the study it was also found thayt female teachers are more accountable towards their job than their male counterparts.

Vandana Mehra, Dilli Raj Newa (2009): "School teachers Attitude towards information and communication technology (ICT)".The present study was conducted to investigate the attitude towards information and communication technology of 300 school teachers of secondary schools of Nepal. The main findings of the study were, private and secondary school teachers exhibited comparable attitude towards ICT. Teachers belonging to different academic streams viz, language, science/mathematics and social sciences exhibited comparable attitude towards ICT

2.2 Perception of Gaps and Linkage of Present Study

It may be seen from the brief reviews of literature presented in the foregoing pages that a few studies have been careied out in the area of Educational Technology. Studies on the relative impact of the each of the severakl independent variables that affect the Educational technology are rare to find. The precised product studies in the area of problems in teaching educational technology are rare to find.

The present study is investigate to fill the gap of the dearth in the exclusive study of teaching learning problems in educational Technology at B.Ed level.

From above reviews it is very clear that there are very few gaps in abroad and Indian reviews of literature. In abroad reviews there is a gap in the year 1996 among learners and among the teacher reviews there is a gap in the years 1998,1999 and 2008.

In Indian reviews of literature there is a gap in the year 1990, 1992,1993,1994,1996 and 2007 among learners and in 1997 , 2007 there is a gap in teacher reviews.

Review of literature reveals that an extensive study of the influence of independent variables and dependent variables are very rare. It is an attempt to see the relationship between the Teaching learning problem in educational technology and the actual content of the educational technology.The area under the investigation is novel and unexplored one with respect to population of B.Ed students and the nature of the work

From the above abroad and Indian reviews of literature it is very clear that no research attempt was made on the presenct study so far hence to fill this gap the researcher has taken up the pre sent study.

Chapter - 3

Methodology

This chapter deals with the various procedures implemented in construction and standardization of the data gathering instruments on different variables. which are included in the study, the methods adopted in the selection of sample, collection of the data, scoring and statically techniques employed.

3.1 Tools of the Study

The following tools are used in the study:

1. Check list cum rating questionnaire to elicit the opinion of the teacher educator about difficulty and intensity level of the problems in teaching educational technology.
2. Check list cum rating questionnaire to elicit the opinion of the student teacher about difficulty and intensity level of the problem in learning educational technology.
3. Personal data sheet.

3.2 Check List along with Intensity Level Eliciting the Opinion of the Teacher Educator about the Difficulty and Intensity Level in Teaching the Educational Technology

The check list cum rating questionnaire contained the 40 statements of teaching Educational Technology by the teacher educator.

Five columns were provided for each statement for rating the difficulty i.e; yes or no and other three columns (i.e., High intensity, moderate intensity, and Low intensity) are given to know ther intensity level on the given problem. The rating questionnaire on the difficulty and intensity in level of the problem in teaching by the Teacher Educator is given in appendix –A.

3.2.1 Construction of the Tool

Previous studies would give an insight into factors by previous investigation, the investigator had consulted the college principals and staff and obtained their views on the Teaching problems in Educational Technology. The investigator consulted the person proficient in English and got their opinion with regard to suitability and ambiguity of the wording of the items. The pool of items thus collected was retained and preliminary form of the questionnaire was prepared with 50 items. The items were included to cover all the variables considered for the study.

3.2.2 Precautions Taken in Constructing the Checklist Cum Rating Questionnaire

Every care was taken that it has all the characteristics of a good ckecklist cum rating questionnaire form.

- The total items in the inventory were 50 only, there by taking roughly only 30-40 minutes for answering the checklist cum rating questionnaire.
- In the usage of the language, care was taken to see that wording of items was as simple and clear as far as possible. The checklist cum rating questionnaire was tried with the help of the Teacher Educators and other friends of the investigation.
- All the items are positively worded statements.

3.2.3 Preperation of Answer Sheet

No Separate Sheet was use for answers. Preperation of answer sheet was very simple and required some time. The items were arranged on a checklist cum rating questionnaire. In the checklist there are yes, no. The numerical values 1,0 were assigned to these alternatives. In the 3 point scale under the assumption that the interval between three alternatives namely High, moderate, low. The numerical values 3, 2, 1 were assigned to these are alternatives depending upon the intensity level.

3.2.4 Pilot Study (Teacher Educator's)

The purpose of the pilot study was to find out whether the items included in the check list cum rating questionnaire were direct relavent and easily understood. The pilot study was planned and carried out with a sample of 20 randomly selected teacher educators representing the teaching at B.Ed level. The questionnaires are

1. Checklist cum rating questionnaire on the difficulty and intensity level of the problem of teaching Educational Technology.
2. The information provided by the teacher educator in the respective colleges were talked. The researcher also paid visits to some of the colleges where the teacher educator selected for to verify the correctness of the information provided by them.

Regarding the items in the questionnaire respondents were requested to express their opinions frankly and freely at the end of the questionnaire thus some in irrelevancies and ambiguities came to light. In the light of this experience and discussions with experts and experienced teachers, slight verbal changes were made in some items in the interest of clarity. No respondent gave any new item under the problem of teaching educational technology further. They commented that the questionnaire was quite exhaustive. The comments of teacher educators and experts on the questionnaire prepared for the study and modifications are carried out.

3.2.5 Item Analysis

Item analysis of the responses of the teacher Educators who participated in the pilot study was carried separately by the method of criterion of internal consistency. The results obtained by this method of criterion internal consistency agree very well with the results of the traditional method of item analysis.

The method consists of rank ordering the respondents with respect to their total scores and taking a high group and low group on the total score and calculating the internal consistency of any statement = mean score of high group – mean score of low group.

On the basis of discriminative power of the items thus obtained, they can be rank ordered and the required number of items with discriminative power can be selected for inclusion in the instrument (Edward , 1939).

In this investigation the highest scoring 27 percent and lowest scoring 27 percent were considered for item analysis as Kelly (1932) found that with 27 percent in each tail the discriminative power is maximum.

3.2.6 Statistics Used for Analysis

The results obtained in item analysis the responses of Teacher Educators are shown in table -3.1.

Table 3.1: Internal consistency of different items

Statement No	d	Statement No	d	Statement No	d	Statement No	d
1	0.46	16	0.61	31	0.66	46	0.49
2	0.39	17	0.58	32	0.42	47	0.66
3	0.53	18	0.40	33	0.17@	48	0.20@
4	0.37	19	0.68	34	0.65	49	0.48
5	0.48	20	0.26@	35	0.69	50	0.65

6	0.44	21	0.54	36	0.74		
7	0.51	22	0.42	37	0.51		
8	0.39	23	0.04@	38	0.78		
9	0.20@	24	0.13@	39	0.65		
10	0.47	25	0.39	40	0.49		
11	0.70	26	0.54	41	0.57		
12	0.09@	27	0.65	42	0.44		
13	0.51	28	0.21@	43	0.30@		
14	0.46	29	0.50	44	0.52		
15	0.17@	30	0.41	45	0.48		

Note: 1. d= difference between the mean scores (high group- low group)

2. @ = items having internal consistency below 0.35

The items have an internal consistency of 0.35 or more were selected .it may be seen form teble -1 that 'd' values below 0.35 for the items 9,12,15,20,23,24,28,33,43 and 48 were therefore eliminated and the remaining 40items consisted for the final form out of 50. The final form of the checklist cum rating questionnaire was given in appendix –B.

3.2.7 Validity

The questionnaire was obtained towards the problems under study. The questionnaire comprised specific and relatively independent question items, each dealing with a specific aspect of overall situation. There fore, the validity of individual items another than that of the whole quotionnaire was considered. It is necessary for each questionnaire to have face validity i.e., each question must be related to the lesson under investigation. There was an adequate coverage of all lessons in the questionnaire. The questions were clean and unambiguous in the questionnaire. All the above mention aspects were taken in establishing the validity of the questionnaire. The questionnaire was administered on a sample of 20 teaching educators of teaching B.Ed level to see whether their response to the questionnaire actually represented their views on the subjects concerned. It was found that their response to the questionnaires actually represented their views on the subjects discussed. Thus, the validity of the of the questionnaires was established. The intrinsic validity of the present checklist cum rating scale was $\sqrt{0.78}$= 0.88

3.2.8 Reliability

The reliability of the questionnaire is difficult to establish with any degree of precession. The usual procedures followed for measuring the reliability of the tests are difficult to adopt in the case of questionnaire. In establishing the reliability of the questionnaires the "test-retest" method was followed because of the independent nature of items. The teacher educator were asked to respond against retest after an interval of 15 days and their answers were compared with those given earlier for consistency of responses.

For the accuracy of the response to the questionnaire an oral interview was conducted and the responses to the interview were compared with those to the questionnaire and were found to be consistent. Thus the reliability of the questionnaire was 0.78

3.3 Check List Along With Intensity Level Eliciting the Opinion of the Student Teacher About the Difficulty and Intensity Level in Learning the Educational Technology

The check list cum rating questionnaire contained the 33 statements of learning Educational Technology by the Student Teacher

Five columns were provided for each statement each for rating the difficulty i.e., yes or no. and other three columns (i.e., High intensity, moderate intensity, and Low intensity) are given to know their intensity level on the problem, The rating questionnaire on the difficulty and intensity in level of the problem in learning by the Student Teacher is given in appendix -C

3.3.1 Construction of the Tool

Previous studies would give an insight into factors by previous investigation, the investigator had consulted the college principals, staff and B.Ed students and obtained their views on the learning problems in Educational Technology. The investigator consulted the person proficient in English and got their opinion with regard to suitability and ambiguity of the wording of the items. The pool of items thus collected was retained and preliminary form of the questionnaire was prepared with 45 items. The items were included to cover all the variables considered for the study.

3.3.2 Precautions Taken in Constructing the Checklist cum Rating Questionnaire

Every care was taken that it has all the characteristics of a good ckecklist cum rating questionnaire form.

- The total items in the inventory were 45 only, there by taking roughly only 30-40 minutes for answering the checklist cum rating questionnaire.

- In the usage of the language, care was taken to see that wording of items was as simple and clear as far as possible. The checklist cum rating questionnaire was tried with the help of the classmates and other friends of the investigation.
- All the items are positively worded statements.

3.3.3 Preperation of Answer Sheet

No Separate Sheet was use for answers. Preperation of answer sheet was very simple and required some time .The items were arranged on a checklist cum rating questionnaire. In the checklist there are yes, no. The numerical values 1,0 were assigned to these alternatives. In the 3 point scale under the assumption that the interval between three alternatives namely High, moderate, low. The numerical values 3, 2, 1 were assigned to these are alternatives depending upon the intensity level.

3.3.4 Pilot Study (Student Teachers)

The purpose of the pilot study was to find out whether the items included in the checklist cum rating questionnaire were direct relevant and easily understood. The pilot study was planned and carried out with a sample of 100 randomly selected student teachers representing the learning at B.Ed level. Care was taken to see that the subjects represented different regions, sex, management ,locality, methodologies etc. The Questionnaires are

- Checklist cum rating questionnaire on the difficulty and intensity level of the problem of level of learning educational technology.
- The information provided by the student teacher in the respective colleges were talked.

Regarding the items in the questionnaire respondents were requested to express their opinions frankly and freely , by assuring them that their responses would be kept confidential and would be used only for research purpose. Thus some irrelevancies and ambiguities came to light. In the light of his experience and discussions with experts and experienced teachers slight verbal changes were made in some items in the interest of clarity. No respondent gave any new item under the problem of learning educational Technology further. They commented that the questionnaire was quite exhaustive. The comments of student teachers and experts on the questionnaire prepared for the study and modifications are carried out.

3.3.5 Item Analysis

Item analysis of the responses of the student teachers who participated in the pilot study was carried separately by the method of criterion of internal consistency. The results obtained by this method of criterion internal consistency agree very well with the results of the traditional method of item analysis.

The method consists of rank ordering the respondents with respect to their total scores and taking a high group and low group on the total score and calculating the internal consistency of any statement = mean score of high group – mean score of low group.

On the basis of discriminative power of the items thus obtained, they can be rank ordered and the required number of items with discriminative power can be selected for inclusion in the instrument (Edward , 1939).

In this investigation the highest scoring 27 percent and lowest scoring 27 percent were considered for item analysis as Kelly (1932) found that with 27 percent in each tail the discriminative power is maximum.

3.3.6 Results If Item Analysis

The results obtained in item analysis the responses of student teachers are shown in table -3.2

Table 3.2: Internal consistency of different items

Statement No	d	Statement No	d	Statement No	d
1	0.49	16	0.51	31	0.04@
2	0.66	17	0.37	32	0.62
3	0.41	18	0.70	33	0.07@
4	0.19@	19	0.07@	34	0.44
5	0.66	20	0.48	35	0.70
6	0.55	21	0.19@	36	0.45
7	0.41	22	0.37	37	0.37
8	0.37	23	0.55	38	0.62
9	0.43	24	0.04@	39	0.04@
10	0.41	25	0.41	40	0.19@
11	0.66	26	0.41	41	0.41
12	0.37	27	0.41	42	0.45
13	0.51	28	0.04@	43	0.36
14	0.70	29	0.40	44	0.47
15	0.70	30	0.04@	45	0.59

Note: 1. d= difference between the mean scores (high group- low group)

2. @ = items having internal consistency below 0.35

The items have an internal consistency of 0.35 or more were selected . it may be seen form teble -1 that 'd' values below 0.35 for the items 4,19,21,

24,28,30,31, 33,39,40 were therefore eliminated and the remaining 35 items consisted for the final form out of 45. The final form of the checklist cum rating questionnaire was given in appendix –D

3.3.7 Validity

The questionnaire was obtained towards the problems under study . The questionnaires comprised specific and relatively independent question items, each dealing with a specific aspect of overall situation. Therefore , the validity of individual items are other than that of the whole questionnaire was considered. It is necessary for each questionnaire to have face validity i.e., each question must be related to the lesson under investigation. There was an adequate coverage of all lessons in the questionnaire .The questions were clear and unambiguous in the questionnaire. All the above mentioned aspects were taken in establishing the validity of the questionnaire. The questionnaire was administered on a sample of 100 student teachers of learning B.Ed level to see whether their response to the questionnaires actually represented their views on the subjects concerned. It was found that their response to the questionnaires actually represented their views on the subjects discussed. Thus, the validity of the questionnaires was established. The intrinsic validity of the present checklist cum rating scale was $\sqrt{0.78}$= 0.88

3.3.8 Reliability

The reliability of the questionnaire is difficult to establish with any degree of precision. The usual procedures followed for measuring the reliability of the tests are difficult to adopt in the case of questionnaire.

In establishing the reliability of the questionnaires the "test-retest" method was followed because of the independent nature of items. The student teachers were asked to respond against retest after an interval of 15 days and their answers were compared with those given earlier for consistency of responses.

For the accuracy of the response to the questionnaire an oral interview was conducted and the responses to the interview were compared with those to the questionnaire and were found to be consistent. Thus the reliability of the questionnaire was 0.78.

3.4 Sample of the Study

Survey Method was found suitable for this study. A sample of 600 student teachers and 200 Teacher Educators was selected by following stratified random sampling.

The study was conducted onf A.P state. The state is geographically divided into 3 regions. They are Rayalaseema, Coastal and Telangana regions. There are 4 districts in Rayalaseema , 9 districts in Coastal and 10 districts in Telangana region. As for education and economy is concerned Andhra region stands in first with an average level of education and economy. All the teaching educators/student teachers in A.P were the universe sample of the present study. The total samples selected under Student Teachers are 600 out of these 200 samples are selected from each region and The total sample selected under Teacher – Education are 200. 100 from Coastal Andra, 50 Telangana and Rayalaseema 50.The Student teachers and teacher educators sampling is shown in table- 3.3 & 3.4.

The sampling technique employed in the present study in selecting the samples were stratified random sampling.

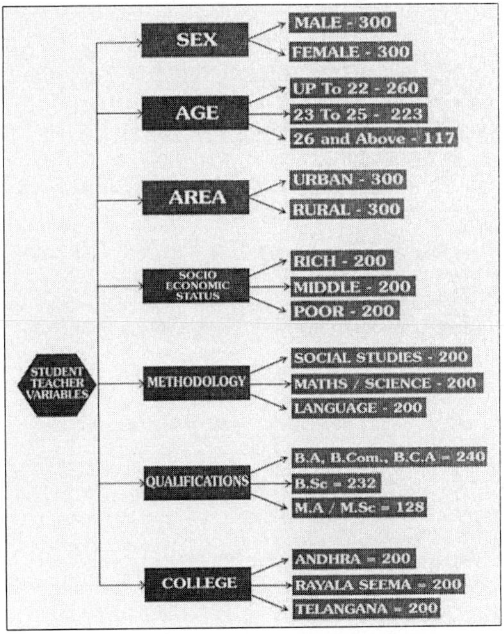

Table 3.3: Sample Design of Student Teachers (600)

S No.	Name of The College	Male	Female	Student Teachers in Andhra Region (200)
1	SSR Coe Chapuram Panchayat, Srikakulam	5	5	
2	Vidyadhari Coe, Besides Lic Office, Srikakulam.	5	5	
3	Gayatri College of Education, Gotlam, Thotapalem	5	5	
4	Shobha Memorial COE, Zami Vizianagaram	5	5	

5	St. Mary Centenary College of Education, Ganapuram,VSP	5	5	
6	Vignana Vihar Coe Gudilova, Vsp	5	5	
7	Benaiah Christian Coe, Burugupudi, Rajahmundry	5	5	
8	S.A.M.D. College of Education for Women, Rajahmundry	5	5	
9	St. Mary Stella Coll. of Edn., Tadepalligudem	5	5	
10	Nova Coll. of Edn., Vegavaram, Jangareddygudem	5	5	
11	Sri M.V. Krishna Rao Coe, Avanigadda	5	5	
12	Kg Prasad Rao & A.N.R. Coe, Gudivada	5	5	
13	ST. Andrews Coe, Vijayawada	5	5	
14	Acharya N.G. Ranga Coll. Of Edn., Chilumuru, Tenali	5	5	
15	R.V.R.R. College OF Education, JKC RD, Guntur	5	5	
16	Sims Coe, Mangaldas Nagar, Guntur	5	5	
17	Priyanka College Of Education, Ongole	5	5	
18	St. Paul's Coe, Giddalur, Prakasam	5	5	
19	Universal Christian Coll. of Education, Nellore	5	5	
20	Vr College of Edn, Nellore	5	5	
Total		100	100	

S No.	Name of the College	Male	Female	
1	St. Lawrence College of Education, Khammam	5	5	Student Teachers in Telangana Region (200)
2	Mother Theresa Coll. of edn., Kothuru, Sathupally	5	5	
3	Viswambara Coll. of Edn., Bollikunta, Sangam (M)	5	5	
4	Sravanthi Coll. of Edn., Dharmaram, Geesugonda (M)	5	5	
5	Surya College Of Education, Jagityal	5	5	
6	Jyothi Coe, Sircilla, Karimnagar	5	5	
7	Karshak B.Ed. College, Kamareddy	5	5	
8	Indur Coe, Bodhan, Nizamabad	5	5	
9	Muduganti Suryamma Coe, Asifabad, Adilabad	5	5	
10	Dr. Rajendraprasad B.Ed. College, Asifabad	5	5	
11	Sidhartha Coe, Bandamidipally, Mahaboobnagar	5	5	
12	Radiance Coe, Moulana Azad Cly, Yenugonda, MBN.	5	5	
13	St. Mary's Coe, Lingareddypally, Siddipet	5	5	
14	Noble Coe, Toopran, Medak Dist	5	5	
15	Sri Krishnadevaray Coe, Kranthi Nagar, Nalgonda	5	5	

16	Mohammeden's Coe, Devarakonda, Nalgonda	5	5	
17	Nav Bharath College of Education, Bolaram	5	5	
18	Iase, Masab Tank, Hyderabad	5	5	
19	Brindavan INST Of Teacher Edn, Sheriguda, Ibrahimpatan	5	5	
20	St. Anns College of Edn. For Women, Malkajgiri, Hyderabad	5	5	
	Total	100	100	

S No.	Name of The College	Male	Female	
1	Azizia College of Education, Adoni	5	5	Student Teachers In Raualaseem a Region (200)
2	St. Peter College of Education, Adoni	5	5	
3	Bharathi Coe, Nandyal	5	5	
4	Viswavani College of Education, Nandyal	5	5	
5	Nalanda College of Education, Yemmiganur	5	5	
6	Sri Rayalaseema Christian Coe,Kurnool	5	5	
7	Tagore Coe, Kodumuru, Knl (Dist)	5	5	
8	Prabhat Coe, Bandiatmakur, Knl	5	5	
9	S.B.V.R. College of Education, Badvel	5	5	
10	Panchaseela Coe, Proddatur, Kadapa	5	5	
11	Sri Annamacharya College of Education, Rajampet	5	5	
12	New Model College of Education, Siddavatam, Kadapa	5	5	
13	Dr. Penubala Penchalaiah Coe, Rly Kodur	5	5	
14	St. Xavier's Coe, Hindupur	5	5	
15	Venkateswara Coe, Kadiri, Anantapur	5	5	
16	Sridevi Coe, Borampalli, Kalyandurg, ATP	5	5	
17	Sri Venkateswara College of Education, Chittoor	5	5	
18	Global Inst. of Advanced Study in Edn., Palamaner	5	5	
19	Sri Venkateswara Coe, Bangarupalem, CTR.	5	5	
20	M Venkata Subba Reddy Coe, Tiruchanur Road, Tirupati	5	5	
Total		100	100	

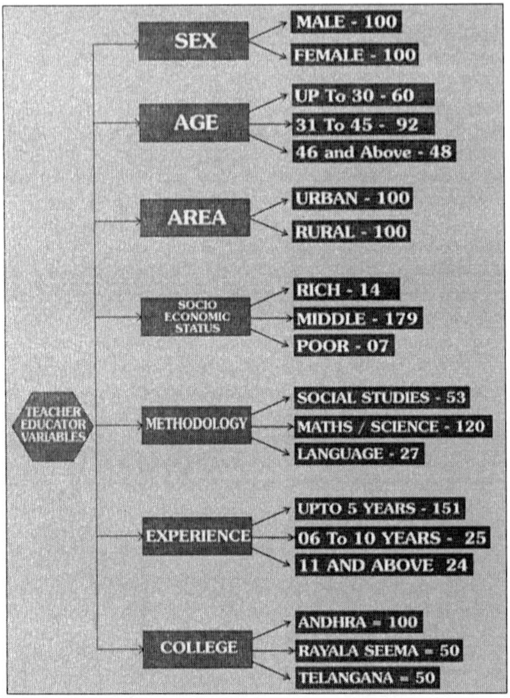

Table 3.4: Sample Design of Teacher Educators (200)

S. No	Name of the College	Male	Female	
1	SSR Coe Chapuram Panchayat, Srikakulam	1	o	Teacher educators in andhra region (100)
2	Vidyadhari Coe, Besides LIC Office,Srikakulam.	1	0	
3	Sri Venkateswara Coe , Etcherla, Srikakulam	0	1	
4	Rangamudri College of Education, Iruvada, Vangara (M)	1	0	
5	Sri Radhakrishna College of Education, Palakonda	0	1	
6	Y Kamala College of Education, Srungavarapu Kota	1	0	
7	Gayatri College of Education, Gotlam, Thotapalem	0	1	
8	Shobha Memorial Coe, Zami Vizianagaram	0	1	
9	Jesus And Mary Coe, Sowbhagyaraya Puram, Pendurthi, VSP	1	0	
10	St. Paul Coe, Singannabanda, Bhemmunipatnam, Vsp	1	0	
11	Dadi Satyanarayana College of Education, Anakapally	1	0	
12	Amg College of Education For Women, Bheemunipatnam	0	1	
13	St. Mary Centenary College of Education,	1	0	

	Ganapuram, VSP			
14	Vignana Vihar Coe Gudilova, VSP	0	1	
15	Dept of Education, Au, Vizag	0	1	
16	Elim College of Education, Amalapuram	1	0	
17	G.B.R. College of Education, Anaparthi	0	1	
18	The Mother's Integral Coe, Aryavatam, Kajuluru, Eg	1	0	
19	Sri Sai Aditya Coe, Jagannaickpur, Kakinada	0	1	
20	SKML Coe, Ramanayyapeta, Kakinada	0	1	
21	Vidyavan Women College of Education, Kakinada	1	0	
22	St. John College of Education, Vistrantipuram Rajahmundry	0	1	
23	VVS Coe, Nagulapalli, U. Kothapalli, EG	1	0	
24	St. Joseph College of Education, Rajahmundry	0	1	
25	Benaiah Christian Coe, Burugupudi, Rajahmundry	1	0	
26	S.A.M.D. College Of Education For Women, Rajahmundry	1	0	
27	Sarada (Gkrao & Vasanthamma) Coe, Pidimgoyya, Rajahmundry	0	1	
28	Smt. Srnm College of Education, Bommuru, Rajahmundry	1	0	
29	Siddartha College of Education, S. Annavaram, Tuni	0	1	
30	Aadi Lakshmi Coe, Navakhandravada, Pithapuram, Eg	1	0	
31	Mohan Coe, Eswar Nagar, Kakinada, Eg	0	1	
32	Venkateswara Coe, Machavaram, Ambajipet, Eg	1	0	
33	KSNR COE, PENMANTRA, WG.	1	0	
34	A.S.R. College of Education, Kovvur	1	1	
35	Sruthi College of Education, Nidadavole	0	1	
36	Nagarjuna Coe, Sankarapuram, Nidadavolu	1	0	
37	Jbeera Coe, Sitarampuram, Narsapuram	0	1	
38	St. Mary Stella Coll. of Edn., Tadepalligudem	1	0	
39	Nova Coll. of Edn., Vegavaram, Jangareddygudem	1	0	
40	Sri Ragahavendra Coe, Narsimhapuram, Bhimvaram	1	1	
41	Indiradevi Coe, Parimpudi, Koyyalagudem, WG	0	1	
42	Sri M.V. Krishna Rao Coe, Avanigadda	1	0	
43	Viswajyothi College of Education, Gudlavalleru	1	1	
44	Kg Prasad Rao & A.N.R. Coe, Gudivada	1	0	
45	Viswavignan College Of Education, Gudivada	1	0	
46	DR. DS Kothari Coe, Jaggayapet	0	1	
47	S.P.M.H. College Of Education For Women, Machilipatnam	1	0	
48	St. Thomas College of Education, Thiruvuru	1	1	
49	Satya Coe, Nadim Tiruvuru	0	1	

50	Montessari Mahila College of Education, Vijayawada	1	0	
51	St. Andrews Coe, Vijayawada	1	1	
52	Acharya N.G. Ranga Coll. of Edn., chilumuru, Tenali	0	1	
53	TRK Coe, Ganapavaram, Chilakaluripet	1	0	
54	GVR & Scoe, Ring RD, Guntur	1	0	
55	R.V.R.R. College of Education, JKCRD, Guntur	1	1	
56	Sims Coe, Mangaldas Nagar,Guntur	0	1	
57	St. Mark NTR College of Education, Narsaraopet	0	1	
58	Repalle Christian College of Education, Repalle	1	0	
59	Nalanda Coe, Kantepudi, Sattenapalli, Guntur	0	1	
60	Vellanki Coe, Sattenapalli	1	0	
61	Bapuji Coe, Tenali	1	0	
62	Ksr & Krk Coe, Burripalem RD, Tenali	1	0	
63	Vinukonda B.ED. College, Kanamarlapudi, Vinukonda	1	0	
64	Anitha Venkateswar Rao Coe, Gangananna Pet, Tenali	0	1	
65	Aman Showkath B.Ed College, Isspalem, Narsaraopet	0	1	
66	Hindu Coe, Opp Sri Venkateswara Vignan Mandir,GTR.	1	1	
67	Ali Coe, NTRRD,Vinukonda, GTR	0	1	
68	Kalikamba College of Education, Chirala	0	1	
69	Ravindrabharathi Coll.of Edn., Kothapeta, Chirala	1	0	
70	Bmrm Jhansi B.Ed College, Addanki, Darsi RD	0	1	
71	Smt. Manaru Yasodamma Memorial B.Ed. College, Darsi	1	0	
72	Sri Venkateswara Coe, Darsi	0	1	
73	Adarsha College of Education, Giddalur	1	1	
74	Chaitanya College of Education, Markapuram	0	1	
75	BA & KR Coe, Medarametla, Prakasam	1	0	
76	Amrutha Coe, Mulaguntapadu, Singarayakonda	0	1	
77	Kamala Coe, Markapur	0	1	
78	Priyanka College of Education, Ongole	0	1	
79	Alfa Coll.of Edn., Kangiri.	0	1	
80	Sri Bvsr Coe, Cheemakurthi, Prakasm Dist	1	0	
81	Sri Chaitanya College of Education, Podili	0	1	
82	Qis College of Education, Pondur RD. Ongole	1	1	
83	Tarlupadu Coll. of Edn., Tarlupadu	0	1	
84	St. Paul's Coe, Giddalur, Prakasam	1	1	
85	Andhra Kesari Coe, Ongole, Prakasam	0	1	
86	D Prameela Mem. Coll. of Edn., A.S. Peta,	1	0	

	Atmakur, (NLR)			
87	C Anil Kumar M. Coe, Gudur, Nellore	1	0	
88	Audishankara Coe, Gudur	1	0	
89	Universal Christian Coll. of Education, Nellore	0	1	
90	VR College of Edn, Nellore	0	1	
	Total	50	50	

S. No	Name of the College	Male	Female	
1	st. Lawrence College of Education, Khammam	1	0	
2	Mother Theresa Coll. of Edn., Kothuru, Sathupally	0	1	
3	St. John's Coe, Aswaraopet, Khammam	1	0	
4	KLR Coe, Paloncha, Khammam	0	1	
5	St Mary College of Education, Jangoan	1	0	
6	Viswambara Coll. of Edn., Bollikunta, Sangam (M)	0	1	
7	Sravanthi Coll. of Edn., Dharmaram, Geesugonda (M)	0	1	
8	St. Peter's College of Education, Hanamkonda	1	0	
9	Educare College of Education, Jangaon	1	0	
10	Yasmeen B.Ed. College, Unikicherla, Dharmasagar (M)	1	0	
11	L.B. College of Education, Warangal	0	1	
12	Sangamitra Coe, Husnabad, KRM	1	0	Teacher Educators in Telangana Region (50)
13	Surya College of Education, Jagityal	0	1	
14	Jyothi Coe, Sircilla, Karimnagar	1	0	
15	Sri Klnr Coe, Jagtial, Karimnagar	0	1	
16	Karshak B.Ed. College, Kamareddy	1	0	
17	Kakatiya B.Ed. College, Nizamabad	0	1	
18	Vijay Coe for Women, Nizamabad	1	1	
19	Indur Coe, Bodhan, Nizamabad	0	1	
20	Vivekananda College of Education, Adilabad	0	1	
21	Muduganti Suryamma Coe, Asifabad, Adilabad	1	0	
22	Dr. Rajendraprasad B.Ed. College, Asifabad	1	0	
23	Viswavikas College of Education, Shadnagar	1	0	
24	Sidhartha Coe, Bandamidipally, Mahaboobnagar	0	1	
25	Radiance Coe, Moulana Azad Cly, Yenugonda, MBN.	1	0	
26	Siddipet Col of Edn, Prasanth Nagar, Siddipet	0	1	
27	GMR Coe, Zaheerabad, Med.	1	1	

28	St. Mary's Coe, Lingareddypally, Siddipet	0	1	
29	Noble Coe, Toopran, Medak Dist	1	0	
30	Sri Venkateswara Coe, Dubbaka, Medak	0	1	
31	Aurora school of Edn., bhongir	1	0	
32	Bhongir College of Education, Bhongir	1	0	
33	Madhava Inst. of Advanced Study in Education, bhongir	0	1	
34	Sri Krishnadevaray Coe, Kranthi Nagar, Nalgonda	0	1	
35	Mohammeden's Coe, Devarakonda, Nalgonda	1	0	
36	Sana Coe, Kodad, Nalgonda	1	0	
37	Vatsalya Coe, Bhongir, Nalgonda	0	1	
38	Nav Bharath College of Education,Bolaram	1	0	
39	St. Mary's Coe, St. Francis St, Secunderabad	0	1	
40	St. Alphonsas Coe, Madhuranagar, Hyderabad	1	0	
41	Iase, Masab Tank, Hyderabad	0	1	
42	Holy Trinity College of Education, Bogaram, Keesara	1	0	
43	Srividya College of Education, Bowrampet, R.R. DT	1	0	
44	Vivekananda Coe, Chevella	0	1	
45	Brindavan Inst of Teacher Edn, Sheriguda, Ibrahimpatan	0	1	
46	St. Anns college of edn. For women, malkajgiri, hyderabad	1	0	
47	Einsten Coll. of edn., Nadergul, Saroornagar (M)	0	1	
48	St. George College of Education, Shankarpally	0	1	
		25	25	

S. No.	Name of the College	Male	Female	
1	Azizia College of Education, Adoni	1	1	Teacher Educators in Rayalaseema Region (50)
2	Sri Balaji College of Education, Adoni	1	0	
3	St. Peter College of Education, Adoni	1	1	
4	Sri Sankaras College of Education, Kurnool	1	0	
5	Bharathi Coe, Nandyal	1	1	
6	GMR Coe, Nandyal	1	1	
7	GM Coe, Nandyal	0	1	
8	Viswavani College of Education, Nandyal	1	0	
9	St. Peter's College of Education, Pathikonda, Kurnool	0	1	

10	Mother Theressa Coll. of Edn., Yemmiganur	1	0	
11	Nalanda College of Education, Yemmiganur	1	0	
12	Sri Rayalaseema Christian Coe, Kurnool	0	1	
13	Tagore Coe, Kodumuru, Knl (Dist)	1	1	
14	Venkataratna Coe, Maruthinagar, Kurnool	1	1	
15	Prabhat Coe, Bandiatmakur, Knl	0	1	
16	Prasad College of Education, DC Rd, KDP.	1	0	
17	S.B.V.R. College of Education, Badvel	0	1	
18	Raja Foundation Coe, Mylavaram, Kadapa Dist	0	1	
19	Panchaseela Coe, Proddatur, Kadapa	1	0	
20	Udaya Sandhya Coe, Korrapadu Rd, Proddatur, Kadapa	1	1	
21	Sri Annamacharya College of Education, Rajampet	0	1	
22	Annamacharya Coll. of Edn., New Boyanapally, Rajampet	1	0	
23	Residency Coe, Rajampet, Kadapa	1	1	
24	Penubala coll. of Edn., Railway Kodur, Kadapa DT.	1	0	
25	New Model College of Education, Siddavatam, Kadapa	0	1	
26	Nirmala Coe, Madras Road, Kadapa	1	1	
27	Dr. Penubala Penchalaiah Coe, Rly Kodur	0	1	
28	St. Xavier's Coe, Hindupur	1	0	
29	Venkateswara Coe, Kadiri, Anantapur	1	1	
30	Sai Siddartha Coe, Tadpatri, Anantapur	1	0	
31	Sridevi Coe, Borampalli, Kalyandurg, ATP	0	1	
32	Sri Venkateswara College of Education, Chittoor	1	0	
33	Global inst. of Advanced Study in Edn., Palamaner	1	1	
34	Vidyalaya College of Education, Tirupathi	1	0	
35	BRM B.Ed College, Kothaindlu, Punganur	0	1	
36	Sri Venkateswara Coe, Bangarupalem, Ctr.	0	1	
37	M Venkata Subba Reddy Coe, Tiruchanur Road, Tirupati	1	1	
38	Christian Coe, Madanapalle	0	1	
Total		25	25	

3.5 Scoring

The procedure of scoring adopted for the checklist cum rating questionnaire list was simply to sum-up the number of ticks given under category of response. The instructions given for each of the questionnaire and checklist are self explanatory to understand the scoring procedure.

3.6 Administration of the Tool

Teaching Learning Problems in Educational Technology was administered to the selected sample of student teachers and Teacher Educators of Andhra, Telangana and Rayalaseema regions.

Permission to collect the data for the study was obtained from the authorities and the investigator met the student teachers studying in those institutions and was informed the importance of research. Though the instrument was self administering one, the necessary instruction were given in the Teaching learning problems in Educational Technology for B.Ed students Questionnaire was made clear to the student teachers and teacher educators and were requested to respond the bio-data form. The student teachers also assured that the data would be used only for research work and would be kept confidential and hence requested to express learning problems intensity level of educational technology. The student teachersand teacher educators were asked to indicate their responses on checklist cum questionnaire by tick, the relevant one.

3.7 Statistical Techniques Employed

The following statistical techniques were employed in the analysis of data collected.

Table 3.5: Statistical Techniques Employed

1	Measures of Central Tendancy	Mean
2	Measures of Variability	Standard Deviation
3	Non-Parametric Test	Chi-Square Test
4	Test of Significance	t-Test and F-Ratio

The significant levels employed with respective symbols are given below:

** indicates significant at 0.01 level

* indicates significant at 0.05 level

@ indicates not significant at 0.05 level.

Chapter - 4

Results and Discussion

The chapter deals with presentation of data, analysis and inter precaution of data.

4.1 Difficulty and Intensity level of the Problems Perceived by the Teacher Educators in Teaching Educational Technology for B.Ed. Level

A check list cum rating questionnaire with five columns were prepared to examine the difficulty and intensity level of the problems in Teaching Educational Technology. For this purpose the Teacher Educators were asked to express their opinions about each statement in the questionnaire whether it was difficult or not. For their response, to know the level of their intensity on the given in the other three columns as high, moderate and low intensity level are given in the questionnaire. Every row was checked by adding the frequencies. Further the data was analyzed and interpreted.

Hypothesis

Their exists no significant differences between the observed intensity level and the expected intensity level of each statement included in the problem of Teaching Educational Technology.

To test the hypothesis chi-square technique was employed in this study for each statement. This procedure was adopted for all the 40 statements included in the questionnaire. If the chi-square value was significant, the frequency contributing most for the significant difference was found out and that statement was confirmed to belong to the level of difficulty.

Table 4.1: Frequencies under different categories of difficulty and intensity level of each of the statement and the value of chi-square (Teacher - Educators).

S No.	Statement	Yes	No	Intensity Level			
				High	Moderate	Low	$\chi2$
1.	Are you facing problem to teach the subject in regional language.	36 (18)	164 (82)	12 (12)	16 (12)	8 (12)	2.66@
2.	While preparation for the	100	100	6	75 (33.3)	19	80.73**

	class, contents cannot digest at once.	(50)	(50)	(33.3)		(33.3)	
3.	Cannot use the technology apparatus appropriately while teaching the points	129 (64.5)	71 (35.5)	21 (43)	71 (43)	37 (43)	30.3**
4.	Problem in using right terminology and also in explanation	95 (47.5)	105 (52.5)	30 (31.6)	46 (31.6)	19 (31.6)	11.64**
5	Problem in clarifying the doubts relating to the subject for some students.	114 (57)	86 (43)	29 (38)	46 (38)	39 (38)	3.84@
6	Facing difficulty in teaching computers due to lack of computer knowledge.	81 (40.5)	119 (59.5)	28 (27)	45 (27)	8 (27)	25.41**
7	Lack of teaching the subject to the student level.	120 (60)	80 (40)	41 (40)	64 (40)	15 (40)	30.03**
8	Facing difficulty in teaching Action Research topic in Educational Technology.	51 (25.5)	149 (74.5)	3 (17)	32 (17)	16 (17)	25.29**
9	Problem in using A.V. aids	68 (34)	132 (66)	5 (22.6)	54 (22.6)	9 (22.6)	65.49**
10	No refreshing courses for the subject lecturers regarding A.V aids.	155 (77.5)	45 (22.5)	70 (51.6)	54 (51.6)	31 (51.6)	14.91**
11	Problem in teaching of some topics in curriculum regarding latest technology.	146 (73)	54 (27)	43 (48.6)	82 (48.6)	21 (48.6)	39.27**
12	Problem in teaching effectively for both practical and theory.	112 (56)	88 (44)	17 (37.3)	63 (37.3)	32 (37.3)	29.49**
13	Problem with lack of equipment in colleges (or) lack of technology resources.	138 (69)	62 (31)	58 (46)	50 (46)	30 (46)	9.03**
14	Proportionate teaching aids are not used with respect to theory.	128 (64)	72 (36)	34 (42.6)	74 (42.6)	20 (42.6)	36.84**
15	Non-availability of adequate equipment in lab.	133 (66.5)	67 (33.5)	29 (44.3)	92 (44.3)	12 (44.3)	80.19**
16	Lack of equipment related to the student strength	147 (73.5)	53 (26.5)	38 (49)	73 (49)	36 (49)	7.65*

	(ratio).						
17	Lack of idea in teaching microteaching skills.	101 (50.5)	99 (49.5)	26 (33.6)	55 (33.6)	20 33.6)	20.82**
18	In most of the cases microteaching cycle process is not followed.	112 (56)	88 (44)	46 (37.3)	52 (37.3)	14 (37.3)	22.35**
19	If we use the microteaching cycle, time is not sufficient for one year course.	133 (66.5)	67 (33.5)	40 (44.3)	50 (44.3)	43 (44.3)	1.17@
20	During the observation of microteaching, teacher educator does not have an idea on classroom interaction.	81 (40.5)	119 (59.5)	20 (27)	38 (27)	23 (27)	6.87*
21	If we have an idea on classroom interaction, time is not sufficient to teach all skills.	155 (77.5)	45 (22.5)	49 (51.6)	91 (51.6)	15 (51.6)	56.16**
22	Skilled teachers are not available for teaching the microteaching.	104 (52)	96 (48)	33 (34.6)	63 (34.6)	8 (34.6)	43.75**
23	For the feed back process in microteaching, required audio-visual equipments are not available.	143 (71.5)	57 (28.5)	56 (47.6)	57 (47.6)	30 (47.6)	1.29@0
24	Are you having right experience to rate the scale of microteaching components	139 (69.5)	61 (30.5)	35 (46.3)	78 (46.3)	26 (46.3)	33.33**
25	Very few microteaching skills are taught in the class, one to not knowing them properly.	117 (58.5)	83 (41.5)	37 (39)	64 (39)	16 (39)	29.67**
26	Most of the teachers while teaching the skills they are not able to perform proportionate movements related to the skill before students	122 (61)	78 (39)	56 (40.6)	50 (40.6)	16 (40.6)	22.89**
27	If the right teacher performs right skill movements the student teacher feels like an entertainment programme.	103 (51.5)	97 (49.5)	47 (34.3)	44 (34.3)	12 (34.3)	21.9**

28	To develop a skill we require minimum 36 minutes. But according the time table time is not permitting for a related lecturer to complete the cycle.	130 (65)	70 (35)	57 (43.3)	65 (43.3)	8 (43.3)	43.95**
29	Lack of idea on technology the teacher not able to teach regarding projected and non projected teaching aids.	93 (46.5)	107 (53.5)	40 (31)	34 (31)	19 (31)	7.53*
30	Most of the lecturers will not have command on transfer of educational technology in methodology content.	87 (43.5)	113 (56.5)	31 (29)	44 (29)	12 (29)	17.82**
31	The educational technology lecturer cannot satisfy the social science students regarding some scientific related topics.	129 (64.5)	71 (35.5)	42 (43)	63 (43)	24 (43)	17.7**
32	There is no proportionate response from the student teacher while teaching the right qualified teacher.	78 (39)	122 (61)	42 (26)	32 (26)	4 (26)	29.82**
33	Basic knowledge on education of a student was not experienced by A.V aids. So a teacher-educator will have the problem in teaching the subject.	139 (69.5)	61 (30.5)	33 (46.3)	66 (46.3)	40 (46.3)	13.05**
34	Most of the teacher educators are confused between hardware and software.	101 (50.5)	99 (49.5)	27 (33.6)	28 (33.6)	46 (33.6)	17.13**
35	Facing difficulty in teaching class room interaction like FAICS, VICS etc.	96 (48)	104 (52)	31 (32)	48 (32)	17 (32)	15.06**
36	Because of short duration of the course the teacher is having maximum problem on analyzing	153 (76)	48 (241)	38 (50.6)	75 (50.6)	39 (50.6)	17.52**

	psychology of the student.						
37	If the micro skills are not taught properly it may affect the macro teaching in methodologies.	141 (70.5)	59 (29.5)	83 (47)	35 (47)	23 (47)	42.87**
38	Facing difficulty in teaching the concept of programming learning.	64 (32)	136 (68)	14 (21.3)	34 (21.3)	16 (21.3)	11.37**
39	Have you taught the computer assisted instruction (CAI) and programmed instruction (PI) without any problem?	119 (59.5)	81 (40.5)	25 (39.6)	65 (39.6)	29 (39.6)	24.48**
40	No teacher is following the principles of demonstration.	145 (72.5)	55 (27.5)	38 (48.3)	56 (48.3)	51 (48.3)	3.54@

Note: 1. Numbers out side the brackets are obtained frequencies & inside the brackets are percentages (%)

2. Numbers inside the brackets are expected frequencies (f_e)

** indicates significant at 0.01 level

* indicates significant at 0.05 level

@ indicates not significant at 0.05 level.

The chi-square value for statement no.s 1,5,19,23 and 40 are not significant at 0.05 level. This reveals that there was no significant difference between the observed and expected difficulty level for the statements.

The following procedure was adopted in this study to retain or to reject a statement. Such of the following statement for which chi-square values were not significant, laid to be no difficulty in teaching Educational Technology.

Results: On the lines of the above procedure the statements felt difficulty by the Teacher Educator given to them in teaching educational Technology.

4.2 Difficulty and Intensity Level of the Problems Perceived by the Student Teacher in Learning Educational Technology for B.Ed. Level.

A check list cum rating questionnaire with five columns were prepared to examine the difficulty and intensity level of the problems in learning Educational Technology. For this purpose the Teacher educators were asked to express their opinions about each statement in the questionnaire whether it was difficult or not. For their response, which level of their intensity was their to listed the other three columns are given as high, moderate and low intensity level in the questionnaire

Every row was checked by adding the frequencies. Further the data was analyzed and interpreted.

Hypothesis

Their exists no significant differences between the observed intensity level and the expected intensity level of each statement included in the problem of learning Educational Technology.

To test the hypothesis chi-square technique was employed in this study for each statement. This procedure was adopted for all the 33 statements included in the questionnaire. If the chi-square value was significant, the frequency contributing most for the significant difference was found out and that statement was confirmed to belong to the level of difficulty.

Table 4.2: Frequencies under different categories of difficulty and intensity level of each of the statement and the value of chi-square (Student - Teachers)

S. No	Statement/Problem	Yes	No	Intensity Level			X^2
				High	Moderate	Low	
1	Students are facing multi problems regarding language which is used by different lecturers who have come from different areas	527 (87.83)	73 (12.17)	37 (175.6)	458 (175.6)	32 (175.6)	680.97**
2	Are you facing the problem in learning the B.Ed subject because it differs from the subjects at graduation within a short duration	487 (81.17)	113 (18.83)	108 (162.3)	329 (162.3)	50 (162.3)	267.06**
3	There is a problem in learning the mechanism of hardware and software	339 (56.5)	261 (43.5)	82 (113)	198 (113)	59 (113)	98.22**
4	Science students are well capable in learning and operating the equipment of technology when	447 (74.5)	153 (25.5)	114 (149)	291 (149)	42 (149)	220.35**

	compared to social students						
5	Some contents are not understood because of wrong explanation by the teacher educator	336 (56)	264 (44)	74 (112)	178 (112)	84 (112)	58.77**
6	If your teachers are not able to clarify your doubts do you feel that educational technology is a difficult subject	478 (79.67)	122 (20.33)	86 (159.3)	247 (159.3)	145 (159.3)	83.28**
7	Do you feel any problem, when your mates are disturbing the classroom during a good lecture?	290 (48.33)	310 (51.67)	103 (96.6)	143 (96.6)	44 (96.6)	51.33**
8	Lecturers are not interested in operating the laboratory equipment	283 (47.17)	317 (52.83)	81 (94.3)	159 (94.3)	43 (94.3)	74.16**
9	Are you not able to adverse with subject computers	281 (46.83)	319 (53.17)	120 (93.6)	122 (93.6)	39 (93.6)	47.91**
10	Some of the lecturers are not able to operate the technology apparatus in classroom/lab.	351 (58.5)	249 (41.5)	82 (117)	174 (117)	95 (117)	42.36**
11	There is a problem of learning the theory in proportionate to practical in educational technology.	424 (70.67)	176 (29.33)	124 (141.3)	270 (141.3)	30 (141.3)	206.97**
12	There is a problem of learning the theory in proportionate to practical in educational technology	492 (82)	108 (18)	205 (164)	220 (164)	67 (164)	86.73**
13	Some of the teachers do not know about the microteaching skills.	425 (54.17)	275 (45.83)	170 (141.6)	183 (141.6)	72 (141.6)	51.99**
14	Because of huge curriculum I am not able to follow all the	373 (62.17)	227 (37.83)	137 (124.3)	160 (124.3)	76 (124.3)	30.3**

	skills of microteaching.						
15	Do you feel difficulty in learning educational technology because unqualified and unrelated subject teachers teach the subject?	352 (58.67)	248 (41.33)	86 (117.3)	212 (117.3)	54 (117.3)	118.95**
16	Do you feel difficult in learning the difference between the different classroom interaction like FAICS,VICS etc.	400 (66.67)	200 (33.33)	143 (133.3)	204 (133.3)	53 (133.3)	86.55**
17	Have you any problem in learning the concept of programme learning?	317 (52.83)	283 (47.17)	69 (105.6)	207 (105.6)	41 (105.6)	149.55**
18	Have you any difficulty in understanding the topic system approach in educational technology?	325 (54.17)	275 (45.83)	77 (108.3)	194 (108.3)	54 (108.3)	104.07**
19	Is computer assisted instruction (CAI) and programmed instruction (PI) are taught by your teacher well?	434 (72.33)	166 (27.67)	164 (144.6)	241 (144.6)	29 (144.6)	159.27**
20	Does your institution has sufficient computers and internet facility?	407 (67.83)	193 (32.17)	121 (135.6)	241 (135.6)	45 (135.6)	143.91**
21	Does your institution provide you in learning the internet and multimedia approach often?	367 (61.17)	233 (38.83)	67 (156)	235 (156)	65 (156)	155.67**
22	Is your institution providing systematic audio lab and language laboratory?	306 (51)	294 (49)	46 (102)	217 (102)	43 (102)	194.49**
23	Are you facing	407	193	119	248	40	162.57**

	problem with Educational technology terminology?	(67.83)	(32.17)	(135.6)	(135.6)	(135.6)	
24	Do you memorize the hierarchy of steps in Dale's cone of experience?	468 (78)	132 (22)	252 (156)	201 (156)	15 (156)	199.47**
25	Are you facing any problem in learning the computer subject (M.S.office) in educational technology?	272 (45.33)	328 (54.67)	52 (90.66)	195 (90.66)	25 (90.66)	184.23**
26	My lecturers are guiding and giving practice in operating hardware equipment.	493 (82.17)	107 (17.83)	131 (164.3)	330 (164.3)	32 (164.3)	280.38**
27	Does your teacher welcome your ideas in learning software development?	465 (77.5)	135 (22.5)	123 (155)	278 (155)	64 (155)	157.62**
28	Are you having a separate computer instructor to operate and teach the computer subject?	445 (74.17)	155 (25.83)	123 (148.3)	279 (148.3)	43 (148.3)	194.25**
29	Are you having educational technology lab & computer lab separately?	454 (75.67)	146 (24.33)	223 (151.3)	210 (151.3)	21 (151.3)	168.93**
30	During your microteaching, did your teacher make it compulsory to follow the 557microteaching cycle?	352 (58.67)	248 (41.33)	127 (117.3)	188 (117.3)	37 (117.3)	98.37**
31	Is microteaching helpful to you in promoting your teaching skills?	557 (92.83)	43 (7.17)	324 (185.6)	217 (185.6)	16 (185.6)	263.46**
32	Are you facing problem in operating projected and non projected teaching aid during your internships?	377 (62.83)	223 (37.17)	70 (125.6)	255 (125.6)	52 (125.6)	201.03**

33	Are you having sufficient material for learning Educational Technology?	452 (75.3)	148 (24.7)	129 (150.6)	281 (150.6)	42 (150.6)	194.28**

Note: 1. Numbers out side the brackets are obtained frequencies & inside the brackets are percentages (%)

2. Numbers inside the brackets are expected frequencies (f_e)

** indicates significant at 0.01 level

* indicates significant at 0.05 level

@ indicates not significant at 0.05 level.

The chi square values for all the 33 statements are significant at 0.01 level. This reveals that there is significant difference between the observed and expected difficulty level for the statements.

The following procedure was adopted in this study to retain or to reject a statement.

Such of the following statement for which chi-square values were not significant, laid to be not difficulty in teaching Educational Technology.

Result

On the lines of above procedure all the statements are significant. Hence the teacher educators are having difficult on these 33 statements as perceived in learning Educational Technology difficultly.

4.3 The Problems Faced by the Teacher Educators in Teaching Educational Technology With Relation to Their Personal Variables

4.3.1 The Problem Statement Relating to the Teaching Educational Technology by the Teacher Educator With Regarding to the Sex

To Know the difference between the male and female on problem relating to teaching Educational Technology to the B.Ed Students. The investigator used t-test and the results are given in table-4.3

Table 4.3: Means, SD's and t-values of problems related to the the teacher educators (N-200) according to their Sex

S. No	Sex	N	Intensity Scores		T-Value
			Mean	SD	
1	Male	100	48.07	12.02	0.129@
2	Female	100	47.84	20.26	

@ not significant at the rate of 0.05

- The means scores of the problems faced by the two groups were found to be male (48.07) and female (47.84) respectively.
- To find out the difference between the mean scores of the two groups, t value (0.129) was found. It is less than the table value at 0.05 level.
- Hence the difference between the two means was considered to be not significant thus the hypothesis was accepted.
- It was concluded that the mean scores of the groups were not significantly different.
- There fore there is no sex difference among the teacher educators on problem relating to teaching educational technology for B.Ed., students.

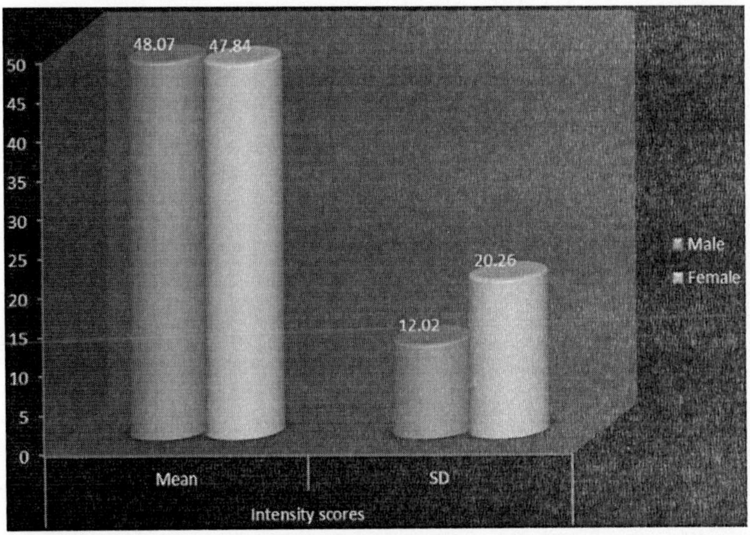

Fig 4.1: Means, SD's of problems related to the teacher educators (N-200) according to their Sex

4.3.2 The Problem Statement Relating to the Teaching Educational Technology by the Teacher Educator With Regarding to the age

To know the difference between the different age groups of the subjects on problem relating to teaching educational technology for B.Ed students, the investigation one way ANNOVA and the results are given in table-4.4.

Table 4.4: ANOVA for problems faced by the Teacher Educators in teaching educational technology (N=200) according to their ages

S. No	Source of Variation	Sum of Squares	DF	Mean Sum of Square	F-Ratio
1	Between the groups	2321.	2	1160.511	4.342 *
2	Within the groups	52657.572	197	267.297	
3	Total	54978.595	199		

* significant at the rate of 0.05

- From table 4.4 the F ratio for problems related by the teaching Educators in teaching educational technology who taught by different subjects for 2 and 197 df is found to be significant at 0.05 level.
- The F ratio was found to be 4.342.
- The significant F ratio indicates that the mean score of different different group of ages taught differ significantly among themselves.
- Hence, the hypothesis that the mean value of the different age groups opted on the problems related to the teacher educators in teaching educational technology differ significantly was not accepted.
- It was inferred that there was significant difference between different age groups taught by Teacher Educators and problem relating to teaching educational technology at B.Ed level.

To find out which of the Age group subjects differ significantly one another the t test was employed.

Table 4.5: Means, SD's and t-value of problems related to the teacher educators (N=200) according to their ages

S. No	Age	N	Intensity Scores		T-Value
			Mean	S.D	
1	Up to 30	60	52.33	18.54	T12=2.82**
2	31 to 45	92	44.49	13.61	T23=1.56 @
3	46 and above	48	49.13	18.16	T13=0.94 @

@ not significant at the rate of 0.05

** significant at the rate of 0.01

From the table -4.5, it could be seen that the problem related to the teacher educators in teaching educational technology scores of mean difference between the age up to 30 years (52.33) and 31 to 45 years (44.49) was significant at 0.01 level. The calculate t12 value was 2.82 .the mean scores of that the age related 31 to 45 was lower than the age up to 30. Hence the hypothesis that subject of different ages (up to 30 and 31to 45 years) did not differ significantly among themselves was rejected it could that there was significant relationship between these two ages with regard to the problem in teaching educational technology.

From the table-4.5, it could be seen that the problem related to the teacher educators in teaching educational technology scores of mean difference between the age 31to 45 years (44.49) and 46 years and above (49.13) was not significant at 0.05 level. The calculate t_{23} value was 1.56 this scores of that the age between 31 to 45 was lower than the age above 46 years .Hence the hypothesis that subject of different ages there was no significant relationship between these two ages with regard to the problem in teaching educational technology did not differ significantly among themselves was accepted. it was concluded that there was no significant relationship between these two ages with regard to the problem in teaching educational technology.

From the table-4.5, it could be seen that the problem related to the teacher educators in teaching educational technology scores of mean difference between the age upto 30 years (52.33) and 46 years and above (49.13) was not significant at 0.05 level. The calculate t_{13} value was 0.94 this scores of that the age above 46 and above was lower than the age up to 30 years .Hence the hypothesis that subject of different ages upto 30 years and above 46 years did not differ significantly among themselves was accepted. it was concluded that there was no significant relationship between these two ages with regard to the problem in teaching educational technology.

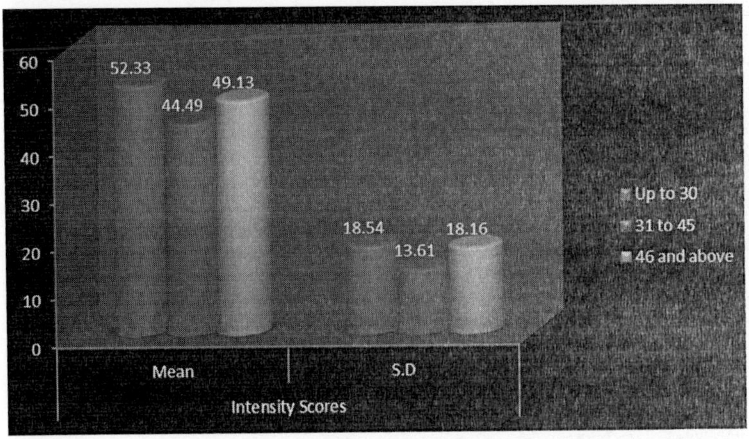

Fig 4.2: Means, SD's and t- values of problems related to the the teacher educators (N-200) according to their Age

4.3.3 The Problem Statement Relating to the Teaching Educational Technology by the Teacher Educator With Regarding to the Area

To Know the difference between the Urban and Rural areas on problem relating to teaching Educational Technology to the B.Ed Students. The investigator used t-test and the results are given in table-4.6

Table 4.6: Means, SD's and T-Values of problems related to the the teacher educators (N-200) according to their area

S. No	Area	N	Intensity scores		T-Value
			Mean	SD	
1	Urban	100	46.6	16.355	1.158 @
2	Rural	100	49.31	16.856	

@ not significant at the rate of 0.05

- The means scores of the problems faced by the two areas were found to be Urban (46.6) and Rural (49.31) respectively.
- To find out the difference between the mean scores of the two areas, t value (1.158) was found. It is less than the table value at 0.05 level.
- Hence the difference between the two means was considered to be not significant thus the hypothesis was accepted.
- It was concluded that the mean scores of the groups were not significantly different. There fore there is no area difference among the teacher educators on problem relating to teaching educational technology for B.Ed., students.

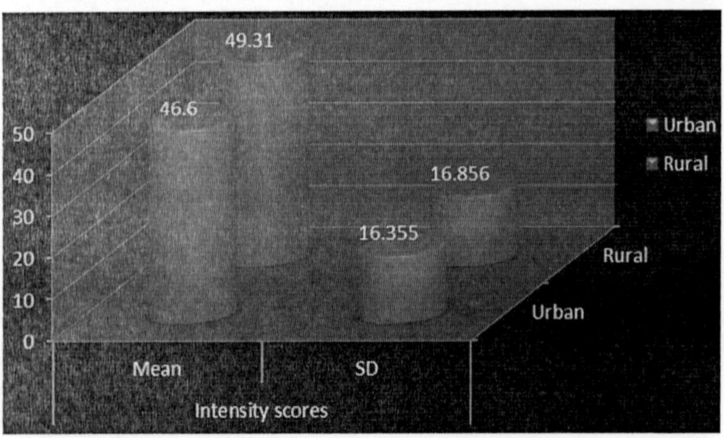

Fig 4.3: Means, SD's of problems related to the the teacher educators (N-200) according to their Area

4.3.4 The Problem Statement Relating to the Teaching Educational Technology By the Teacher Educator With Regarding to the Subjects Taught.

To know the difference between the different subjects taught by teacher educators relating to teaching educational technology for B.Ed students, the investigation one way ANNOVA and the results are given in table-4.7

Table 4.7: ANOVA for problem faced by the Teacher Educators in teaching educational technology (N=200) according to their subjects taught

S. No	Source of Variation	Sum of Squares	DF	Mean Sum of Squares	F- Ratio
1	Between the groups	329.33	2	164.66	0.59@
2	Within the groups	54649.25	197	277.40	
3	Total	54976.59	199		

@ not significant at the rate of 0.05

- From table 4.7 the F ratio for problems related by the teaching Educators in teaching educational technology who taught by different subjects for 2 and 197df was not significant at 0.05 level.
- The F ratio was found to be 0.59.
- The non- significant F ratio indicates that the mean score of different subject taught did not differ significantly.
- Hence, the hypothesis that the mean value of the different group subjects belonging to different subjects taught by the teacher educators in teaching educational technology did not differ significantly was accepted.
- It was inferred that there was no significant difference between different subjects taught by Teacher Educators and problem relating to teaching educational technology at B.Ed level.

4.3.5 The Problem Statement Relating to the Teaching Educational Technology By the Teacher Educator With Regarding to the Experience.

To know the difference between the different experiences of the subjects on problem relating to teaching educational technology for B.Ed students, the investigator use one way ANOVA and the results are given in table-4.8

Table 4.8: ANOVA for problem faced by the Teacher Educators in teaching educational technology (N=200) according to their experience

S. No	Source of Variation	Sum of Squares	DF	Mean Sum of Squares	F-Ratio
1	Between the groups	553.92	2	276.96	1.002@
2	Within the groups	54424.67	197	276.26	
3	Total	54978.59	199		

@ not significant at the rate of 0.05

- From table 4.8 the F ratio for problems related to teaching teaching educational technology related to different experiences for 2 and 197 df was not significant at 0.05 level.
- The F ratio was found to be 1.002. The non- significant F ratio indicates that the mean score of different groups of experience did not differ significantly.
- Hence, the hypothesis that the mean value of the different group of subjects related to different experiences on problem faced by the teacher educators in teaching educational technology did not differ significantly was accepted.
- It was inferred that there was no significant difference between different experiences of teacher educators related to teaching educational technology at B.Ed level.

4.3.6 The Problem Statement Relating to the Teaching Educational Technology By the Teacher Educator With Regarding to the Colleges of Education.

To know the difference between the different colleges of education of the subjects on problem relating to teaching educational technology for B.Ed students, the investigation one way ANOVA and the results are given in table-4.9

Table 4.9: ANOVA for problem faced by the Teacher Educators in teaching educational technology (N=200) according to college of education's.

S No.	Source of Variation	Sum of Squares	df	Mean Sum of Squares	F-Ratio
1	Between the groups	895.85	2	447.93	1.632@
2	Within the groups	54082.74	197	274.53	
3	Total	54978.59	199		

@ not significant at the rate of 0.05.

- From table 4.9 the F ratio for problems relating to teaching educational technology by the Teacher Educators at different colleges for 2and 197 df was not significant at 0.05 level.

- The F ratio was found to be 1.632.
- The non-significant F ratio indicates that the mean scores of different groups of college did not differ significantly.
- Hence, the hypothesis that the mean value of the different group of subjects belonging to different colleges of education in teaching educational technology did not differ significantly was accepted.
- It was inferred that there was no significant difference between the teacher educators teaching in difference colleges of education and the problems related to teaching educational technology.

4.3.7 The Problem Statement Relating to the Teaching Educational Technology By the Teacher Educator With Regarding to the Socio Economic Status.

To know the difference between the different qualifications of the subjects on problem relating to teaching educational technology for B.Ed students, the investigation one way ANNOVA and the results are given in table-4.10

Table 4.10: ANOVA for problems faced by the teacher educators in teaching educational technology (N=200) according to their Socio economic status.

S. No	Source of Variation	Sum of Squares	df	Mean Sum of Squares	F-Ratio
1	Between the groups	4441.51	2	2220.755	8.657**
2	Within the groups	50537.085	197	256.533	
3	Total	54978.595	199		

** significant at the rate of 0.01

- From table 4.10 the F ratio for problems related to the teacher educators in teaching educational technology at different socio economic status for 2 and 197df was found to be significant at 0.01 level.
- The F ratio was found to be 8.657.
- The significant F ratio indicates that the mean score of different group of socio economic status in different levels are significant..
- Hence, the hypothesis that the mean value of the different groups of subject belonging to different socio economic status in teaching educational technology differ significantly was not accepted (i.e., rejected).
- It was inferred that there was significant difference between different socio economic status and problem related to the teacher educators in teaching educational technology

To find out which of the socio economic status differ significantly from one another the t test was employed.

Table 4.11: Means, SD's and t-value of problems related to the teacher educators (N=200) classified According to their socio economic status

S. No	Socio Economic Status	N	Intensity Scores		'T' Value
			Mean	S.D	
1	Rich	14	55.14	13.48	T12=2.263*
2	Middle class	179	46.54	16.38	T13=3.07**
3	poor	7	69.85	8.32	T23=6.916 **

* significant at 0.05 level

** significant at 0.01 level

- From Table 4.11, it could be seen that the problem related to the student teacher in teaching educational technology scores of mean difference between the socio economic status in Rich(55.14) and middle class (46.54) levels are significant at 0.05level.
- The calculated t12 value was 2.263
- This scores that the socio economic status level middle class was lower than the Rich.
- Hence the hypothesis that the teachers of different levels of socio economic status(rich and middle class) differ significantly among themselves was rejected.
- It was concluded that there was significant relationship between these two socio economic status levels with regard to the problem in teaching educational technology.
- From Table 4.11, it could be seen that the problem related to the student teacher in teaching educational technology scores of mean difference between the socio economic status in Rich(55.14) and poor (69.85) levels are significant at 0.01 level.
- The calculated t_{13} value was 3.07.
- This scores that the socio economic status level rich was lower than the poor.
- Hence the hypothesis that the teachers of different levels of socio economic status(rich and poor class) differ significantly among themselves was rejected.
- it was concluded that there was significant relationship between these two socio economic status levels with regard to the problem in teaching educational technology.

- From Table 4.11, it could be seen that the problem related to the student teacher in teaching educational technology scores of mean difference between the socio economic status in middle class (46.54)and poor(69.85) levels are significant at 0.01 level.
- The calculated t_{23} value was 6.916
- This scores that the socio economic status level of middle class was lower than the poor.
- Hence the hypothesis that the teachers of different levels of socio economic status (middle class and poor) differ significantly among themselves was rejected.
- It was concluded that there was significant relationship between these two socio economic status levels with regard to the problem in teaching educational technology.

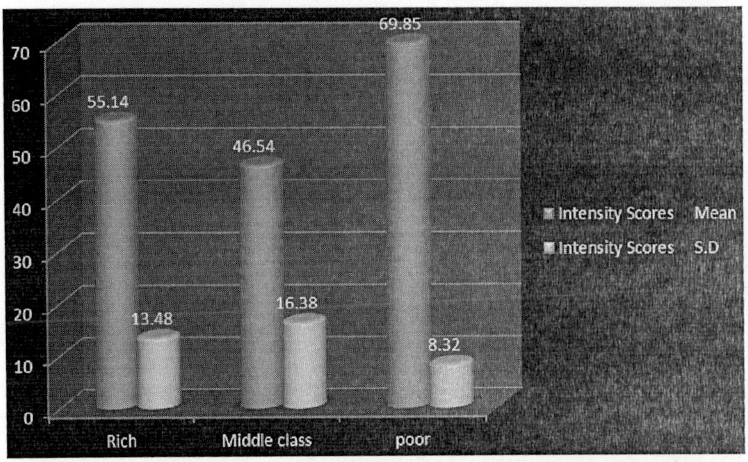

Fig 4.4: Means, SD's of problems related to the the teacher educators (N-200) according to their Socio Economic Status

4.4 The Problems Faced By the Student Teachers in Learning Educational Technology with Relation to Their Personal Variables

4.4.1 The Problem Statement Relating to the Learningg Educational Technology By the Student Teachers With Regarding to the Sex

To know the difference between the male and female on problem relating to learning Educational Technology by the B.Ed Students. The investigator used t-test and the results are given in table-4.12.

Table 4.12: Means, SD's and t-values of problems related to the student teacher (N-600) according to their Sex.

S. No	Sex	N	Intensity Scores		T-Value
			Mean	SD	
1	Male	300	47.87	10.549	0.87@
2	Female	300	47.08	11.576	

@ not significant at the rate of 0.05

- The means scores of the problems related to the tlearning by the two groups were found to be Male(47.87)and Female(47.08)respectively.
- To find out the difference between the mean scores of the two groups, t value (0.87) was found. It was less than the table value at 0.05 level.
- Hence the difference between the two means was considered to be not significant, thus the hypothesis was accepted.
- It was concluded that the mean scores of the groups were not significantly different.
- Therefore there is no significant difference among the student teacher s on problem relating to learn educational technology at B. Ed level.

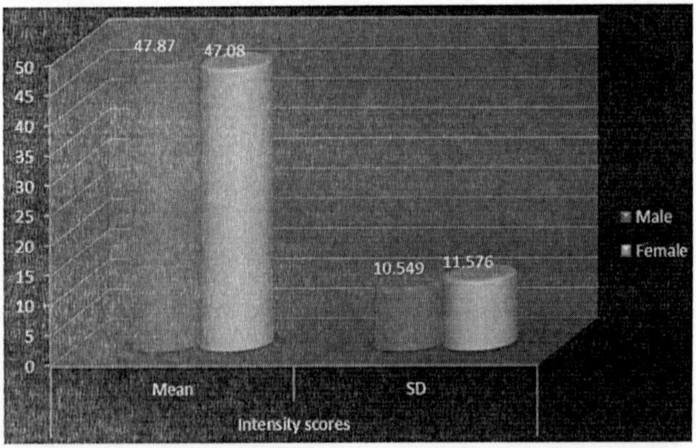

Fig 4.5: Means, SD's of problems related to the student teachers (N-600) according to their Sex

4.4.2 The Problem Statement Relating to the Learning Educational Technology by the Student Teachers with Regarding to their age.

To know the difference between the different age of the subjects on problem relating to learning educational technology for B.Ed students, the investigator use one way ANOVA and the results are given in table-4.13.

Table 4.13: ANOVA for problem faced by the student teachers in Learning educational technology (N=600) according to their age

S. No	Source of Variation	Sum of Squares	DF	Mean Sum of Squares	F-Ratio
1 2 3	Between the groups Within the groups Total	510.07 72929.69 73439.76	2 597 599	255.035 122.16	2.088@

@ not significant at the rate of 0.05

- From the table-4.13 the F ratio for problems related to the student teacher in learning educational technology at different for age levels 2 and 597 df was found to be not significant at 0.05 level.
- The F ratio was found to be 2.088.
- The non -significant F ratio indicates that the mean score of different groups' age did not differ significantly.
- Hence, the hypothesis that the mean values of the different groups of subjects belonging to different age levels on problems faced by the student teachers in learning educational technology did not differ significantly was accepted.
- It was inferred that there was no significant difference between age levels problem related to the learning educational technology by the learners at B.Ed level.

4.4.3 The Problem Statement Relating to the Learning Educational Technology by the Student Teachers with Regarding to the Colleges of Educations in Different Regions.

To know the difference between the different colleges of education of the subjects on problem relating to learning educational technology by B.Ed students, the investigation one way ANOVA and the results are given in table-4.14.

Table 4.14: ANOVA for problem related to the student teachers in learning educational technology (N=600) according to college of education's.

S. No.	Source of Variation	Sum of Squares	DF	Mean Sum of Squares	F-Ratio
1 2 3	Between the groups Within the groups Total	1883.88 71555.88 73439.76	2 597 599	941.94 119.86	7.859 **

** significant at the rate of 0.01

- From table 4.14 the F ratio for problems related to the students teachers in learning educational technology at different colleges for 2 and 597df was found to be significant at 0.01 level.

- The F ratio was found to be 7.859.
- The significant F ratio indicates that the mean score of different group of college in different regions are significant.
- Hence, the hypothesis that the mean value of the different groups of subject belonging to different colleges of education in teaching educational technology differ significantly was not accepted (i.e., rejected).
- It was inferred that there was significant difference between different colleges of education and problem related to the student teachers in learning educational technology.
- To find out which of the qualifications of subject differ significantly from one another the t test was employed.

Table 4.15: Means, SD's and t value of problems related to the student teachers (N=600) classified According to their college of education opted in different regions

S. No	College of Education in Different Regions	N	Intensity Scores		'T' Value
			Mean	S.D	
1	Andhra	200	49.37	10.99	T12=1.258@
2	Rayalaseema	200	47.96	11.53	T13=4.018**
3	Telangana	200	45.11	10.28	T23=2.617 **

@ Not significant at the rate of 0.05

** significant at 0.01 level

- From Table 4.15, it could be seen that the problem related to the student teacher in learning educational technology scores of mean difference between the College of education in Andhra(49.37) and Rayalaseema (47.96) regions were not significant at 0.05 level.
- The calculated t12 value was 1.258. This scores that the College of education in Rayalaseema was lower than the Andhra.
- Hence the hypothesis that the learnrs of different college of Education(Andhra and Rayalaseema)did not differ significantly among themselves was accepted.
- It was concluded that there was no significant relationship between these two regions with regard to the problem in learning educational technology.
- From Table 4.15, it could be seen that the problem related to the student teacher in learning educational technology scores of mean

difference between the College of education in Andhra(49.37) and Telangana (45.11) regions are significant at 0.01 level.

- The calculated t13 value is 4.018
- This scores that the College of education in Telangana was lower than the Andhra.
- Hence the hypothesis that the learnrs of different college of Education(Andhra and Telangana) differ significantly among themselves was rejected.
- It was concluded that there was significant relationship between these two regions with regard to the problem in learning educational technology.
- From Table 4.15, it could be seen that the problem related to the student teacher in learning educational technology scores of mean difference between the College of education in Rayalaseema (47.96) and Telangana (45.11) regions are significant at 0.01 level.
- The calculated t23 value is 2.617
- This scores that the College of education in Telangana was lower than the Rayalaseema
- Hence the hypothesis that the learnrs of different college of Education(Rayalaseema and Telangana) differ significantly among themselves was rejected.
- it was concluded that there was significant relationship between these two regions with regard to the problem in learning educational technology.

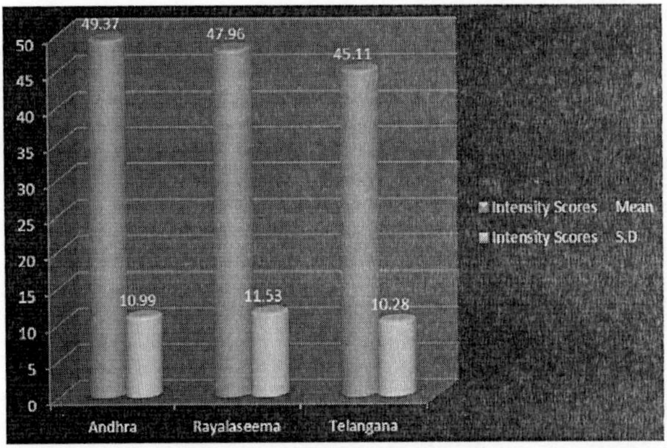

Fig 4.6: Means, SD's of problems related to the student teachers (N-600) according to their Regions

4.4.4 The Problem Statement Relating to the Learning Educational Technology By the Student Teachers With Regarding to Their Qualification.

To know the difference between the different qualifications of the subjects on problem relating to learning educational technology by the B.Ed students, the investigation used one way ANOVA and the results are given in table-4.16.

Table 4.16: ANOVA for problems related to the student teachers in learning educational technology (N=600) according to their qualification.

S. No	Source of Variation	Sum of Squares	DF	Mean Sum of Squares	F-Ratio
1	Between the groups	1090.38	2	545.19	
2	Within the groups	72349.38	597	121.18	4.499*
3	Total	73439.76	599		

** significant at the rate of 0.05

- From table 4.16 the F ratio for problems related to the student teachers in learning educational technology at different qualifications for 2 and 597df was found to be significant at 0.05 level.
- The F ratio was found to be 4.499.
- The significant F ratio indicates that the mean score of different group of qualification are significant.
- Hence, the hypothesis that the mean value of the different groups of subjects belonging to different qualifications on the problem to related to the student teacher in learning educational technology differ significantly was not accepted.
- It was inferred that there was significant difference between different qualifications and problem related to the student teachers in learning educational technology.

To find out which of the qualifications of subject differ significantly from one another the t test was employed

Table 4.17: Means, SD's and t value of problems related to the student teachers in learning (N=600) according to their qualifications

S. No	Qualification	N	Intensity Scores		'T' Value
			Mean	S.D	
1	BA/Bcom/BCA	240	48.48	10.91	T12=2.576*
2	B.Sc	232	45.78	11.87	T13=0.174@
3	M.A/M.Sc	128	48.67	9.44	T23=2.535*

@ not significant at the rate of 0.05

* Significant at 0.05 level

** Significant at 0.01 level

- From Table 4.17, it could be seen that the problem related to the student teacher in learning educational technology scores of mean difference between the qualification B.A/B.com/ BCA (48.48) and B.Sc. (45.78) was significant at 0.05 level.
- The calculated t12 value was 2.576.
- This scores that the qualification B.Sc was lower than the B.A/B.com/ BCA.
- Hence the hypothesis that the subjects of different qualification (B.A/B.com/ BCA and B.Sc.) differ significantly among themselves was rejected.
- It is concluded that there was significant relationship between these two qualification with regard to the problem in learning educational technology.
- From Table 4.17, it could be seen that the problem related to the student teacher in learning educational technology scores of mean difference between the qualification B.A/B.com/BCA (48.48) and M.A/MSc.(48.67) was not significant at 0.05 level.
- The calculated t13 value was 0.174. This scores that the qualification B.A/B.com/ BCA was lower than the M.A/ M.Sc.
- Hence the hypothesis that the subjects of different qualification (B.A/B.com/ BCA and M.A/M.Sc) did not differ significantly among themselves was accepted.
- It is concluded that there was no significant relationship between these two qualification with regard to the problem in learning educational technology.
- From Table 4.17, it could be seen that the problem related to the student teacher in learning educational technology scores of mean difference between the qualification B.Sc (45.78) and M.A/MSc.(48.67) was significant at 0.05 level.
- The calculated t23 value was 2.535.
- This scores that the qualification B.Sc was lower than the M.A/ M.Sc.
- Hence the hypothesis that the subjects of different qualification (B.Sc and M.A/M.Sc) differ significantly among themselves was rejected.
- It is concluded that there was significant relationship between these

two qualification with regard to the problem in learning educational technology.

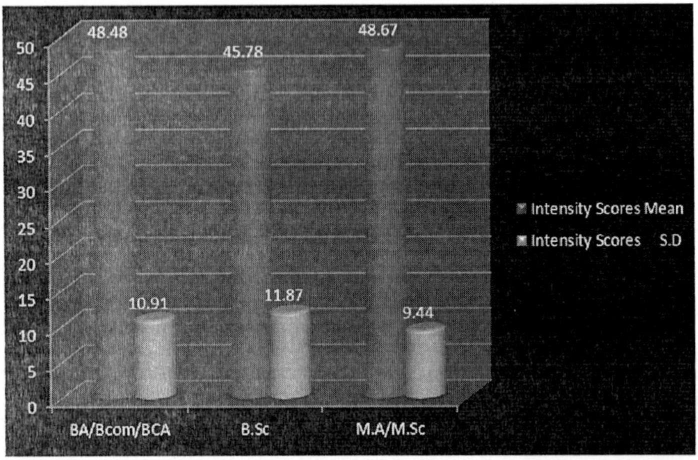

Fig 4.7: Means, SD's of problems related to the student teachers (N-600) according to their Qualification

4.4.5 The Problem Statement Relating to the Learning Educational Technology by the Student Teachers with Regarding to Methodologies Opted.

To know the difference between the different methodologies opted of the subjects on problem relating to learning educational technology by the B.Ed students, the investigator used one way ANOVA and the results are given in table-4.18.

Table 4.18: ANOVA for problem related student teachers (N=600) according to their methodologies opted

S.No	Source of Variation	Sum of Squares	DF	Mean Sum of Squares	F- Ratio
1	Between the groups	2147.816	2	1073.908	8.993**
2	Within the groups	71291.944	597	119.417	
3	Total	73439.76	599		

* significant at the rate of 0.01

- From table 4.18 the F ratio for problems related to the student teachers in learning educational technology at different Methodologies opted for 2 and 597df was significant at 0.01 level.
- The F ratio was found to be 8.993.
- The significant F ratio indicates that the mean score of different groups of Methodologies opted significantly among themselves.

- Hence, the hypothesis that the mean value of the different groups of subjects belonging to different Methodologies opted on the problem to related to the student teacher in learning educational technology differ significantly was not accepted.
- It was inferred that there was significant difference between different Methodologies opted and problem related to the student teachers in learning educational technology

To find out which of the qualifications of subject differ significantly from one another the t test was employed.

Table 4.19: Means, SD's and t-value of problems related to the student teacher (N=600) classified According to their methodologies opted

S. No	Qualification	N	Intensity Scores		'T' Value
			Mean	S.D	
1	Mat/Phy/Eng	200	45.16	9.238	T12=2.528*
2	Bio.Scie &Eng/Tel	200	47.795	11.501	T13=4.325**
3	Soc.studies&Eng/Tel	200	49.485	11.91	T23=1.44@

@ Not significant at the rate of 0.05

* significant at 0.05 level

** significant at 0.01 level

- From Table 4.19, it could be seen that the problem related to the student teacher in learning educational technology scores of mean difference between the Mat/Phy/Eng (45.16) and Bio science & Eng/Tel (47.795) Methodologies opted was significant at 0.05 level.
- The calculated t12 value was 2.528.
- This scores that the Methodologies Mat/Phy/Eng was lower than the Bio Science and Eng/Tel.
- Hence the hypothesis that the subjects of different Methodologies (Mat/Phy/Eng and Bio Science /Eng/Tel).Did differ significantly among themselves was rejected.
- It was concluded that there was significant relationship between these two Methodologies with regard to the problem in learning educational technology.
- From Table 4.19, it could be seen that the problem related to the student teacher in learning educational technology scores of mean difference between the Mat/Phy/Eng (45.16) and Social Science and Eng/Tel (49.485) Methodologies opted was significant at 0.01 level.
- The calculated t13 value was 4.325.

- This scores that the Methodology Mat/phy/Eng was lower than the Social studies and Eng/Tel.
- Hence the hypothesis that the subjects of different Methodology (Mat/phy/Eng and Social studies and Eng/Tel) differ significantly among themselves was rejected.
- It was concluded that there was significant relationship between these two Methodologies with regard to the problem in learning educational technology.
- From Table 4.19, it could be seen that the problem related to the student teacher in learning educational technology scores of mean difference between the Bio science and Eng/Tel(47.795) and Social studies and Eng/Tel(49.485) Methodologies opted was not significant at 0.05 level.
- The calculated t23 value was 1.44.
- This scores that the Methodology Bio Science and Eng/Tel was lower than the social studies and Eng/Tel.
- Hence the hypothesis that the subjects of different Methodologies (Bio Science and Eng/Tel and social science and Eng/Tel) did not differ significantly among themselves was accepted.
- It could that there was no significant relationship between these two Methodology with regard to the problem in learning educational technology.

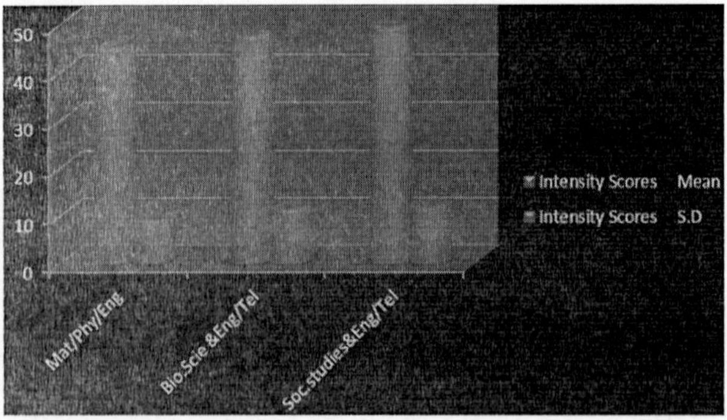

Fig 4.8: Means, SD's of problems related to the student teachers (N-600) according to their methodologies opted

4.4.6 The Problem Statement Relating to the Learning Educational Technology By the Student Teacher with Regarding to the Area

To know the difference between the Urban and Rural areas on problem relating to learning Educational Technology by the B.Ed Students. The investigator used t-test and the results are given in table-4.20

Table 4.20: Means, SD's and t-values of problems related to the student teachers (N-600) according to their area

S. No	Sex	N	Intensity Scores		T-Value
			Mean	SD	
1	Urban	300	49.11	12.61	3.56**
2	Rural	300	45.94	9.04	

** significant at 0.01 level

- The means scores of the problems related to the learning by the two groups were found to be Urban (49.11) and Rural (45.94) respectively.
- To find out the difference between the mean scores of the two groups, t value (3.56) was found. It was significant at 0.01 level.
- Hence the difference between the two means was considered to be significant, thus the hypothesis was rejected.
- It was concluded that the mean scores of the groups were significantly different.
- Therefore there is significant difference among the student teachers on problem relating to learn educational technology at B.Ed level.

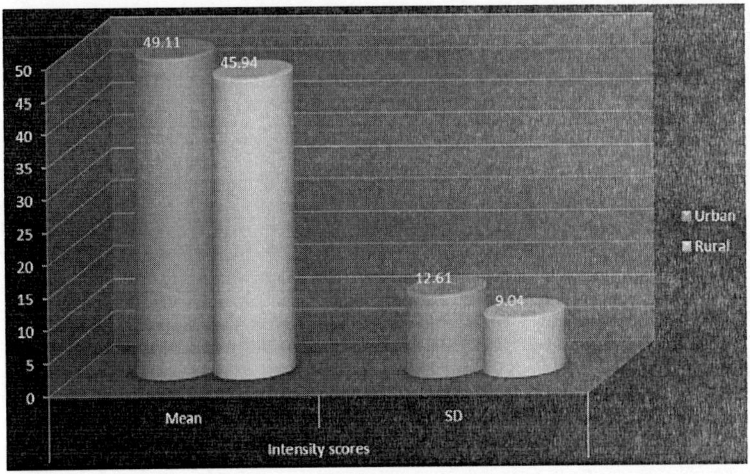

Fig 4.9: Means, SD's of problems related to the student teachers (N-600) according to their area

4.4.7 The Problem Statement Relating to the Learning Educational Technology by the Student Teachers with Regarding to their Socio-Economic Status.

To know the difference between the different colleges of education of the subjects on problem relating to learning educational technology by B.Ed students, the investigation one way ANOVA and the results are given in table-4.21.

Table 4.21: ANOVA for problem related to the student teachers in learning educational technology (N=600) according to their Socio Economic status

S No.	Source of Variation	Sum of Squares	DF	Mean Sum of Squares	F-Ratio
1	Between the groups	4019.61	2	2009.805	17.284**
2	Within the groups	69420.15	597	116.282	
3	Total	73439.76	599		

** significant at the rate of 0.01

- From table 4.21. the F ratio for problems related to the student teachers in learning educational technology at different socio economic status for 2 and 597df was found to be significant at 0.01 level.
- The F ratio was found to be 17.284.
- The significant F ratio indicates that the mean score of different group of socio economic status in different levels are significant.
- Hence, the hypothesis that the mean value of the different groups of subject belonging to different socio economic status in learning educational technology differ significantly was not accepted (i.e., rejected).
- It was inferred that there was significant difference between different socio economic status and problem related to the student teachers in learning educational technology

To find out which of the socio economic status differ significantly from one another the t test was employed.

Table 4.22: Means, SD's and t-value of problems related to the student teacher (N=600) classified According to their socio economic status

S. No	Socio Economic Status	N	Intensity Scores		'T' Value
			Mean	S.D	
1	Rich	200	49.135	11.35	T12=4.678**
2	Middle class	200	43.825	11.45	T13=0.332@
3	poor	200	49.48	9.43	T23=5.416 **

@ Not significant at the rate of 0.05

** significant at 0.01 level

- From Table 4.22, it could be seen that the problem related to the student teacher in learning educational technology scores of mean difference between the socio economic status in Rich (49.135) and middle class (43.825) levels are significant at 0.01 level.
- The calculated t12 value was 4.678.
- This scores that the socio economic status level middle class was lower than the Rich.
- Hence the hypothesis that the learnrs of different levels of socio economic status(rich and middle class) differ significantly among themselves was rejected.
- It was concluded that there was significant relationship between these two socio economic status levels with regard to the problem in learning educational technology.
- From Table 4.22, it could be seen that the problem related to the student teacher in learning educational technology scores of mean difference between the socio economic status in Rich(49.135) and poor (49.48) levels are not significant at 0.05 level.
- The calculated t13 value was 0.32.
- This scores that the socio economic status level rich was lower than the poor.
- Hence the hypothesis that the learners of different levels of socio economic status (rich and poor class) did not differ significantly among themselves was accepted.
- It was concluded that there was no significant relationship between these two socio economic status levels with regard to the problem in learning educational technology.
- From Table 4.22, it could be seen that the problem related to the student teacher in learning educational technology scores of mean difference between the socio economic status in middle class (43.825) and poor (49.48) levels are significant at 0.01 level.
- The calculated t23 value was 5.416
- This scores that the socio economic status level of middle class was lower than the poor.
- Hence the hypothesis that the learners of different levels of socio economic status (middle class and poor) differ significantly among themselves was rejected.

- It was concluded that there was significant relationship between these two socio economic status levels with regard to the problem in learning educational technology.

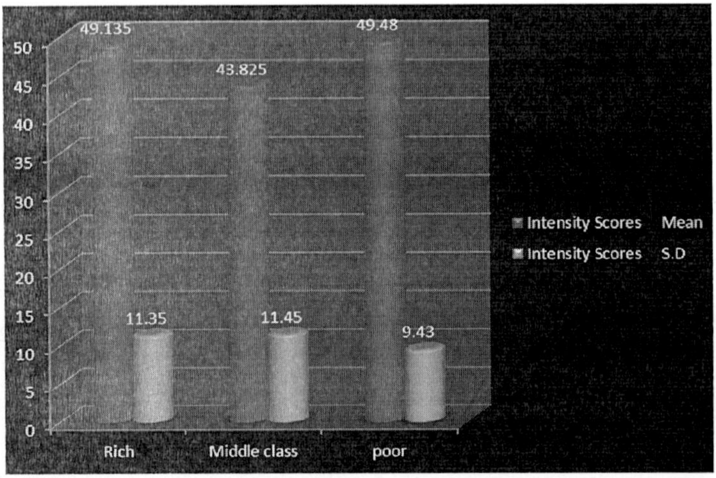

Fig 4.10: Means, SD's of problems related to the student teacher (N=600) classified According to their socio economic status

Chapter - 5

Major Findings, Conclusions and Suggetions for Further Research

5.1 Major Findings

1. The statement no.s 1,5,19,23 and 40 are not significant at 0.05 level. This reveals that there was no significant difference between the observed and expected difficulty level for the statements.
2. 35 statements are identified as difficult in teaching education technology as perceived by the teacher educator.
3. All the 33 statements are significant at 0.01 level. This reveals that there is significant difference between the observed and expected difficulty level for the statements.
4. All the 33 statements are identified as difficult in learning education technology as perceived by the student teacher.
5. There is no sex difference among the teacher educators on problem relating to teaching educational technology for B.Ed., students.
6. There was significant difference between different age groups taught by Teacher Educators and problem relating to teaching educational technology at B.Ed level.
7. There was significant relationship between these two ages up to (30 and 31to 45 years) with regard to the problem in teaching educational technology.
8. There was no significant relationship between these two ages (31to 45 and above 46 years) with regard to the problem in teaching educational technology.
9. There was no significant relationship between these two ages (up to 30 years and above 46) with regard to the problem in teaching educational technology.
10. There is no area difference among the teacher educators on problem relating to teaching educational technology for B.Ed., students.
11. There was no significant difference between different subjects taught

by Teacher Educators and problem relating to teaching educational technology at B.Ed level.

12. There was no significant difference between different experiences of teacher educators related to teaching educational technology at B.Ed level.
13. There was no significant difference between the teacher educators teaching in difference colleges of education and the problems related to teaching educational technology.
14. There was significant difference between different socio economic status and problem related to the teacher educators in teaching educational technology.
15. There was significant relationship between these two socio economic status levels(rich and middler class) with regard to the problem in teaching educational technology.
16. That there was significant relationship between these two socio economic status levels (rich and poor) with regard to the problem in teaching educational technology.
17. That there was significant relationship between these two socio economic status levels (middle class and poor) with regard to the problem in teaching educational technology.
18. There is no significant difference among the student teachers on problem relating to learn educational technology at B.Ed level.
19. There was no significant difference between age levels problem related to the learning educational technology by the learners at B.Ed level.
20. There was significant difference between different colleges of education and problem related to the student teachers in learning educational technology.
21. There was no significant relationship between these two regions (Andhra and Rayalaseema) with regard to the problem in learning educational technology.
22. There was significant relationship between these two regions (Andhra and Telangana) with regard to the problem in learning educational technology.
23. There was significant relationship between these two regions (Rayalaseema and telangana) with regard to the problem in learning educational technology.

24. There was significant difference between different qualifications and problem related to the student teachers in learning educational technology.
25. There was significant relationship between these two qualification (B.A/B.com/BCA and B.Sc.) with regard to the problem in learning educational technology.
26. There was no significant relationship between these two qualification (B.A/B.com/ BCA and M.A/M.Sc) with regard to the problem in learning educational technology.
27. There was significant relationship between these two qualification (B.Sc and M.A/M.Sc) with regard to the problem in learning educational technology.
28. There was significant difference between different Methodologies opted and problem related to the student teachers in learning educational technology.
29. There was significant relationship between these two Methodologies (Mat/Phy/Eng and Bio Science/Eng/Tel). with regard to the problem in learning educational technology.
30. That there was significant relationship between these two Methodologies(Mat/phy/Eng and Social studies and Eng/Tel) with regard to the problem in learning educational technology.
31. There was no significant relationship between these two Methodology (Bio Science and Eng/Tel and social science and Eng/Tel) with regard to the problem in learning educational technology.
32. There is significant difference among the student teachers of area (Urban and rural) on problem relating to learn educational technology at B.Ed level.
33. There was significant difference between different socio economic status and problem related to the student teachers in learning educational technology.
34. There was significant relationship between these two socio economic status levels(rich and middle class) with regard to the problem in learning educational technology.
35. There was no significant relationship between these two socio economic status levels(rich and poor class) with regard to the problem in learning educational technology.

36. There was significant relationship between these two socio economic status levels (middle class and poor) with regard to the problem in learning educational technology.

5.2 Conclusions

From the above findings the following conclusions are made:

Problems relating to teaching educational technology as perceived by the teacher educators as follows Teacher educator problems

S. No	Statement
1.	While preparation for the class, contents cannot digest at once.
2.	Cannot use the technology apparatus appropriately while teaching the points
3.	Problem in using right terminology and also in explanation
4.	Facing difficulty in teaching computers due to lack of computer knowledge.
5.	Lack of teaching the subject to the student level.
6.	Facing difficulty in teaching Action Research topic in Educational Technology.
7.	Problem in using A.V. aids
8.	No refreshing courses for the subject lecturers regarding A.V aids.
9.	Problem in teaching of some topics in curriculum regarding latest technology.
10	Problem in teaching effectively for both practical and theory.
11	Problem with lack of equipment in colleges (or) lack of technology resources.
12	Proportionate teaching aids are not used with respect to theory.
13	Non-availability of adequate equipment in lab.
14	Lack of equipment related to the student strength (ratio).
15	Lack of idea in teaching microteaching skills.
16	In most of the cases microteaching cycle process is not followed.
17	During the observation of microteaching, teacher educator does not have an idea on classroom interaction.
18	If we have an idea on classroom interaction, time is not sufficient to teach all skills.
19	Skilled teachers are not available for teaching the microteaching.
20	Are you having right experience to rate the scale of microteaching components
21	Very few microteaching skills are taught in the class, one to not knowing them properly.
22	Most of the teachers while teaching the skills they are not able to perform proportionate movements related to the skill before students
23	If the right teacher performs right skill movements the student teacher feels like an entertainment programme.
24	To develop a skill we require minimum 36 minutes. But according the time table time is not permitting for a related lecturer to complete the cycle.
25	Lack of idea on technology the teacher not able to teach regarding projected

	and non projected teaching aids.
26	Most of the lecturers will not have command on transfer of educational technology in methodology content.
27	The educational technology lecturer cannot satisfy the social science students regarding some scientific related topics.
28	There is no proportionate response from the student teacher while teaching the right qualified teacher.
29	Basic knowledge on education of a student was not experienced by A.V aids. So a teacher-educator will have the problem in teaching the subject.
30	Most of the teacher educators are confused between hardware and software.
31	Facing difficulty in teaching class room interaction like FAICS, VICS etc.
32	Because of short duration of the course the teacher is having maximum problem on analyzing psychology of the student .
33	If the micro skills are not taught properly it may affect the macro teaching in methodologies.
34	Facing difficulty in teaching the concept of programming learning.
35	Have you taught the computer assisted instruction (CAI) and programmed instruction (PI) without any problem?

Problems Relating to Learning Educational Technology as Perceived by the Student Teachers Given as Follows

S. No	Statement/Problem
1	Students are facing multi problems regarding language which is used by different lecturers who have come from different areas
2	Are you facing the problem in learning the B.Ed subject because it differs from the subjects at graduation within a short duration
3	There is a problem in learning the mechanism of hardware and software
4	Science students are well capable in learning and operating the equipment of technology when compared to social students
5	Some contents are not understood because of wrong explanation by the teacher educator
6	If your teachers are not able to clarify your doubts do you feel that educational technology is a difficult subject
7	Do you feel any problem, when your mates are disturbing the classroom during a good lecture?
8	Lecturers are not interested in operating the laboratory equipment
9	Are you not able to adverse with subject computers
10	Some of the lecturers are not able to operate the technology apparatus in classroom/lab.
11	There is a problem of learning the theory in proportionate to practical in educational technology.
12	There is a problem of learning the theory in proportionate to practical in educational technology
13	Some of the teachers do not know about the microteaching skills.

14	Because of huge curriculum I am not able to follow all the skills of microteaching.
15	Do you feel difficulty in learning educational technology because unqualified and unrelated subject teachers teach the subject?
16	Do you feel difficult in learning the difference between the different classroom interaction like FAICS, VICS etc.
17	Have you any problem in learning the concept of programme learning?
18	Have you any difficulty in understanding the topic system approach in educational technology?
19	Is computer assisted instruction (CAI) and programmed instruction (PI) are taught by your teacher well?
20	Does your institution has sufficient computers and internet facility?
21	Does your institution provide you in learning the internet and multimedia approach often?
22	Is your institution providing systematic audio lab and language laboratory?
23	Are you facing problem with Educational technology terminology?
24	Do you memorize the hierarchy of steps in Dale's cone of experience?
25	Are you facing any problem in learning the computer subject (M.S.office) in educational technology?
26	My lecturers are guiding and giving practice in operating hardware equipment.
27	Does your teacher welcome your ideas in learning software development?
28	Are you having a separate computer instructor to operate and teach the computer subject?
29	Are you having educational technology lab & computer lab separately?
30	During your microteaching, did your teacher make it compulsory to follow the 557microteaching cycle?
31	Is microteaching helpful to you in promoting your teaching skills?
32	Are you facing problem in operating projected and non projected teaching aid during your internships?
33	Are you having sufficient material for learning Educational Technology?

1. The personal variables related to teacher educators namely sex, area, college, qualification, subjects taught and teaching experience, colleges of education are not impact on their intensity level score of problems relating to teaching educational technology.
2. The personal variable related to Teacher Educators namely age, and socio economic status are impact on the intensity level score of problems relating to teaching education technology.
3. The personal variable related to students teachers namely sex and age are not impact on their intensity level score of problems relaters to learning education technology.
4. The personal variable related to students teachers namely colleges of

education, qualification, methodologies adopted, area and socio economic status are impact on the intensity level score of problems relating to learning education technology.

5.3 Educational Implications

The quality of a nation depends upon the quality of its citizens, the quality of citizens depends upon the quality of their education, the quality of education depends upon the quality of teachers and the quality of teachers depends upon the quality of 'teacher education' among many other factors.

In framing 'teacher education curriculum' one has to keep in mind the constitutional goals, social and economic challenges, political and cultural scenario, scientific and technological revolutions, educational challenges, new emerging concerns, etc.

Kothari Education Commission (1964-66) observed that 'a sound programme of professional education for teachers is essential for the qualitative improvement of education. Investment in teacher education can yield very rich dividends because the financial resources required are small compared with the resulting improvement in the education of millions'.

The teacher serves the humanities and helps to shape the destiny of the society. The teacher has a powerful and abiding influence in the formation of the character of the future citizens. The teacher acts as a pivot for the transmission of intellectual and technical skills and cultural traditions from one generation to another. Hence, effective training has to be provided to the student-teachers at B.Ed level. On the basis of the results of this investigation, the following recommendations are made.

1. Age has influence on the intensity level score of problems relating to learning education technology of B.Ed. students. To provide relevant programmes for lower age teacher educators.
2. Socio – economic status has influence on the intensity level score of problems relating to learning education technology of teacher eductors. Government has to take necessary steps for give eminities and physical facilities may be provided to the teacher educators on the basis of socio – economic status of the teacher educators.
3. Colleges of education has influence on the intensity level score of problems relating to learning education technology of B.Ed. students. Necessary infra - structural facilities and physical facilities may be created in B.Ed. colleges. Congenial atmosphere may be developed in B.Ed. colleges.

4. Student educational qualification has influence on the intensity level score of problems relating to learning education technology of B.Ed. students. Special programmes and special coaching may be provided for B.Ed. students.

5. Methodology has influence on the intensity level score of problems relating to learning education technology of B.Ed. students. Special coaching may be provided for social studies students.

6. Area has influence on the intensity level score of problems relating to learning education technology of B.Ed. students. The Government should take necessary steps to give some concessions to various areas.

7. Socio – economic status has influence on the intensity level score of problems relating to learning education technology of B.Ed. students. Government has to take necessary steps for give scholarships and hostel facilities may be provided to the poor students on the basis of socio – economic status of the students.

5.4 Suggestions for Further Research

1. The prevent investigation is taken on problems relating to teaching hearing educational technology. It may further research on impact of students achievement.

2. It is a sample study for few colleges of education. It may also for other colleges of education in Andhra Pradesh and other states too.

3. The fools used in the prevent study in the present investigation are lot standardized because of paucity of time. It is suggested that standardized tools should be developed.

4. Very few personal and demographical variable are taken up for the present study to get more information about the study other. Personal and demographical variables may be included.

5. The problems relating to teaching and leaving educational technology are alone. Studied other problems also be studied to improves the studies further.

References

1. Abbas ZW. Attitude towards using computers among Malaysian teacher education students world conference on computers in education VI: (WCCE95) liberating the learner London, Scturyn, 1995, 1997, 153-162.

2. Adeline Du Toit, Marie-Luce Muller. Training Competitive Intelligence Analysts via the Web: The University of Johannesburg Experience. Journal of Education for Library and Information Science. 2005; 46(4):320-32.

3. Adriano CT, Shrock SA. Teachers' competence, affect, familiarity, and perceived skill regarding instructional technology. Proceedings of selected research and development presentations at the national convention of the Association for Educational Communications and Technology, sponsored by the Research and Theory Division, February 16-20, Nashville, TN. (ERIC Document Reproduction Service No. ED 373 699), 1994.

4. Agency for Instructional Technology. A survey of the use of technology with students at risk of school failure. Bloomington, IN: Author. (ERIC Document Reproduction Service No. ED 295 591), 1987.

5. Aiex NK. Using Film, Video, and TV in the class room ERIC Clearinghourse on Reading, English, and Communication Digest # 36, November, 1988. Retrieved December 30, 2003 from: http://eric. indiana.edu/ieo/digests/d36.html.

6. Albion P. Setting course for the new millennium: Planning for ICT in a New Bachelor Degree Program. In Society for Information Technology and Teacher Education International Conference, San Diego: California, February 8-12, 2000.

7. Anil Tanaji Patil, Development of Multimedia Instructional System on Computer Education for B.Ed. Pupil Teachers Abstracts of Research Studies Conductedby Teacher Education Institutions in IndiaD.R. Goel, Chhaya Goel, R.L. Madhavi CASE, The M.S. University of Baroda, Vadodara - 390 002, 2006.

8. Anjali Khirwadkar. Developing a computer software for learning Chemistry at Standard IX. CASE, The M.S. University of Baroda,

Vadodara - 390 002, 1999.

9. Munther Mohammed Zyoud. Development of Computer Assisted English Language Teaching for VIII StandardStudents CASE, The M.S. University of Baroda,Vadodara, 1999.

10. Anshuman Das. Exploring effectiveness of computer assisted learning material on Rhymes in different modes CASE, The M.S. University of Baroda, Vadodara-390 002, 1998.

11. Atkinson S. Does the need for high levels of performance curtail the development of creativity in design and technology project work? International Journal of Technology and Design Education. 2000; 10(3):255-281.

12. Baenen N *et al.* Improving achievement through technology: Status report on the Magnet Schools Assistance Program (MSAP) (E & R Report No. 95 E.05). Raleigh, NC: Wake County Public Schools System, Department of Evaluation and Research. (ERIC Document Reproduction Service No. ED 384 342), 1995.

13. Barowy B, Laserna C. (March). The role of the Internet in the adoption of computer modeling as legitimate high school science. Journal of Science Education and Technology. 1997; 6:3-13.

14. Bassoppo-Moyo, Temba C. Evaluating eLearning: A Front-end, Process and Post Hoc Approach. International Journal of Instructional Media, V. 2006; 33(1):7-22.

15. Bates PJ. T-learning study: A study into TV-based interactive learning to the home. Final report for the European community under the IST Programme (1998-2002). Pjp Associates, 2003. Retrieved on December 29, 2003, from http://www.pjb.co.uk/t-learning/ contents.htm.

16. Baylor A, Ritchie D. What factors facilitate teachers skill, teacher morale and perceived student leaving in technology using class room? Computers and Education. 2002; 39(1):395-414.

17. Becker HJ. Analysis and Trends of School Use of Information Technologies. Report for the U.S. congress Office of Technology Assessment, 1994. Retrieved December 30, 2003 from: http://www. gse.uci.edu/doehome/EdResource/Publications/EdTechUse/C-BLCNT.HTM.

18. Beena Desai Y. A Comparative Study of the Efficacy of Teaching Through the Traditional Method and the Multimedia Approach in the

Subject of Home Science CASE, The M.S. University of Baroda, Vadodara , 2004.

19. Bernauer JA. Integrating technology into the curriculum. First year evaluation. Paper presented at the meeting of the American Educational Research Association, San Francisco, CA. (ERIC Document Reproduction Service No. ED 385 224), 1995.

20. Bhalla CL. Atma & Sons. Audio visual aids in educations, Delhi-6, 1963.

21. Bhattacharya M. ed. Special Issue on E-Learning Prospective in Asia Pacific. International Journal on Elearning. 2002; 1(3):5-6, 23-70.

22. Bialo E, Sivin-Kachala J. Effectiveness of technology in schools. Washington, DC: Software Publishers Association, 1995.

23. Bork A. (Fall). Is technology-based learning effective? Contemporary Education, (ERIC Document Reproduction Service No. EJ 443 831). 1991; 63:6-14.

24. Bracey G. (April). New pathways: Technology's empowering influence on teaching. Electronic Learning, 1993, 8-9.

25. Bransford J. (Fall). Learning with technology: Theoretical and empirical perspectives. Peabody Journal of Education. 1986; 64:5-26.

26. Broere Geyser HC, Kruger M. Technology Development: Imperatives for Higher Education. South African Journal of Higher Education. 2002; 16(3):5-12.

27. Brophy J. Interactions of male and female students with male and female teachers. In L. Wilkinson & C. Marrett (Eds.), Gender influences in classroom interactions. Orlando, FL: Academic Press, 1985, 115-142.

28. Bullock, Moving from theory to practice: An examination of the factors that perservice- teachers encounter as they attempt to gain experience teaching with technology during field placement experience. Journal of technology and teacher education. 2004; 12(2):211-237.

29. Butzin SM. (March). Whatever happened to Project CHILD? Learning and Leading with Technology 24, 1997, 24-27.

30. Cameron Richards. Distance Education, On-Campus Learning, and E-Learning Convergences: An Australian Exploration. International Journal on E-Learning. 2002; 1(3):30-9.

31. Carol Chan KK, Ming Fai Pang. Teacher Collaboration in Learning

Communities. Teaching Education (Columbia, S.C.). 2006; 17(1):1-5.

32. Chantahiem Chamnan. A Study of Availability And Utilization of Educational Media in Secondary Schools of Thailand CASE, The M.S. University of Baroda, Vadodara, 2004.

33. Chauhan SS. Innovations in Teaching-learning process, Vikas Publishing Housel; Pvt. Ltd, 5, New Delhi, 1979.

34. Cheryl Brown, Laura Czerniewicz. Access for all? Unpacking the complexities of access to ICTs for diverse South African higher education students. Paper for World Forum on the Information Society.November, 2005.

35. Chidambaram. conducted a study on "Technical Knowledge of teachers in using audio-visual equipment in Mandal Praja Parishad School in Andhra Pradesh. Experimental Education, 1996.

36. Collins A. *et al.* Three different views of students: The role of technology in assessing student performance (Technical Report No. 12). New York: Center for Technology in Education. (ERIC Document Reproduction Service No. ED 337 150), 1991.

37. Cotton K. Computer-assisted instruction. Northwest Regional Educational Laboratory, 1992. Retrieved October 26, 2001, from http://www.nwrel.org/scpd/sirs/5/cu 10.html.

38. Cradler J. Implementing technology in education, 1996. Recent findings from research and evaluation studies [Online]. Available: http://www.wested.org/ techpolicy/ recapproach.html

39. Cradler J, Bridgforth E. Recent research on the effects of technology on teaching and learning [Online], 1996. Available: http://www.wested.org/ techpolicy/research.html

40. Daniel Alemneh G, Samantha Hastings K. Developing the ICT Infrastructure for Africa: Overview of Barriers to Harnessing the Full Power of the Internet. Journal of Education for Library and Information Science. 2006; 47(1):4-16.

41. Darshana Chaudhari. Techno-pedagogic analysis of children ETV programmes and their effectiveness in terms of achievement with and without discussion and perception of students and teachers The M.S. University of Baroda, 2005.

42. Davidson GV, Ritchie SD. How do attitudes of parents, teachers, and students affect the integration of technology into schools? A case study.

Proceedings of Selected Research and Development Presentations at the National Convention of the Association for Educational Communications and Technology Sponsored by the Research and Theory Division 16th, Nashville, TN. (ERIC Document Reproduction Service No. ED 373 710), 1994.

43. Dibakar Sarangi. Exploring cognitive map formed due to educational video viewing among learners. CASE, The M.S. University of Baroda, Vadodara - 390 002, 2000.

44. Dos RC. Educational Technology-A Bank Text, Sterling Publishers, L-10, Green Park Extension, New Delhi-110 016, 1973.

45. Dwyer DC *et al*. The evolution of teachers' instructional beliefs and practices in high-access-to-technology classrooms. Paper presented at the annual meeting of the American Education Research Association, Boston, MA, 1990.

46. Edgar dale, Audio visual methods in teaching. Holt Renehard and Winston, New York, 1961.

47. Ediger. conducted a study of Education in technology. Un published master in education dissertation, 1996.

48. Edward Meyen L, Ron Aust, John Gauch M. e-Learning: A Programmatic Research Construct for the Future. Journal of Special Education Technology. 2002; 17(3):37-46.

49. Eggleston J. Teaching and learning design and technology: A guide to recent research and its application. London: Continuum, 2000.

50. Elijah Omwenga I. A Training Needs Assessment Study on the use of Information and Communications Technologies (ICT) in supporting the provision of Science and Engineering Educationin Five East African Universities. Paper, 2004, 106.

51. Elizabeth A, White Shelly, Wepner B, Donna Wetzel C. Accessible Education Through Assistive Technology. T.H.E. Journal, 2003; 30(7):24-32.

52. Elmer R. Meta-cognition and design and technology education. The Journal of Design and Technology Education. 2002; 7(1):19-24.

53. Ely DP *et al*. Trends in educational technology: Syracuse, NY: ERIC Clearinghouse on Information and Technology, 1995.

54. Flecknoe M. How can ICT Help us to improve Education? Innovations

in Education & Teaching International. 2002; 39(4):271-280.

55. Follansbee S *et al.* Can online communications improve student performance? Results of a controlled study. ERS-Spectrum. 1997; 15:15-26.

56. Fui Tong LEE, Boon Han YEAP. The Use of Educational Technologies in University Teaching & Learning International Conference on Multimedia and ICT in education, 22-24 April, Lisbon, Portugal, 2009. www.formatex.org/micte2009/

57. Garrison R, Anderson T. E-Learning in the 21st Century: A Framework for Research and Practice. Routledge Falmer, London, 2003.

58. Gautam A Panchal. Development and Tryout of Self- learning Materials in English subject on the unit of 'Active and Passive Voice' for the Students of Standard-XII The M.S. University of Baroda, Vadodara - 390 002, 2006.

59. Grassl R, Mingus T. Using technology to enhance problem solving and critical thinking skills. Mathematics and Computer Education. 1997; 31:293-300.

60. Haugland S. Computers and young children. Will technology change early childhood education? Day Care & Early Education. 1995; 22:45-46.

61. Henning Patzold. Increasing Value Without Increasing Effort? The Use of WebCT in Accompanying Face-to-Face Lectures Under the Constraint of Low Budget. Journal of Distance Education. 2005; 20(2):78-84.

62. Hiralkumar M Barot. A study of the effectiveness of CAI in Sanskrit for std. VIII students The M.S. University of Baroda, Vadodara, 2005.

63. Howey K, Zimpher N. Professors and deans of education. In W. R.Houston (Ed.), Handbook of research on teacher education. New York: Macmillan, 1990, 349-390.

64. Interactive Educational System Design. Report on the effective ness of technology in schools, Washington, DC: Software Publishers Association, 1995, 96-96.

65. International Technology Education Association. Where to get a degree in technology education, 2002. Retrieved May 1, 2002, from http://www.iteawww.org/J4.html.

66. Irfan Shah. ICT awareness, use and need of secondary and higher secondary teachers of English Medium Schools of Vadodara city The M.S. University of Baroda, Vadodara - 390 002, 2005.

67. Irshad Hussain, Prof. Dr. Muhammad Aslam (July): Role of mobile technology in promoting campus-wide learning environment The Turkish Online Journal of Educational Technology-Tojet July, 2005, 2009, 8(3). ISSN: 1303-6521 Article 6.

68. Fresen JW, Boyd LG. Caught in the Web of Quality. International Journal of Educational Development. 2005; 25(3):317-331.

69. Jackson D *et al.* Internet resources for middle school science: Golden opportunity or "Silicon snake oil"? Journal of Science Education and Technology. 1997; 6:49-57.

70. Jackson P. Life in the classroom. New York: Holt, Rinehart & Winston, 1968.

71. Jacobson MJ, Levin JA. Network learning environments and hypertext: Constructing personal and shared knowledge spaces. In D. Foster & D. V. Jolly (Eds.), Proceedings of Tel-Ed '93 Dallas, TX: International Society for Technology in Education, 1993, 190-197

72. James Poon TF, JJNG. Students perceptions of Mathematics and design and Technology Unpublished master in education dissertation, 1991.

73. Jaykumar Rathod. Development and Implementation of an Information Technology Based Instructional Package for English Grammar to Gujarati medium students of Standard VIII of Jamnagar City" Abstracts of Research Studies Conductedby Teacher Education Institutions in India Dr. Goel, Chhaya Goel, Madhavi Case RL, The M.S. University of Baroda, Vadodara - 390 002, 2005. file:///D|/research%20abstracts/drg1.htm11/20/2006.

74. Jean Chen. Educational Technology in Introductory College Physics Teaching and Learning: The Importance of Students' Perception and Performance Beyond Boundaries Conference, October 24, 2003.

75. Jegede OJ. Computers and the learning of biological concepts: Attitudes and achievement of Nigerian students. Science Education. 1991; 75:701-706.

76. Jenny Leach. Do New Information and Communication Technologies Have a Role to Play in Achieving Quality Professional Development for Teachers in the Global South? Curriculum Journal, 2005, 16(3):293-

329.

77. John Hedberg G, Lim Cher Ping. Charting Trends for E-Learning in Asian Schools. Distance Education. 2004; 25(2):199-213.

78. John Mativo M. The Challenge of Teaching Technology in a Developing Nation. Tech Directions. 2005; 65(5):22-5.

79. Jonassen DH. Computers as cognitive tools: Learning with technology, not from technology. Journal of Computing in Higher Education. 1995; 6:40-73.

80. Jordan WR, Follman JM. Using technology to improve teaching and learning. Hot Topics: Usable Research. Palatka, FL: NEFEC/SERVE, Regional Vision for Education. (ERIC Document Reproduction Service No. ED 355 930), 1993.

81. Joy BHH, Manickam LSS. Computer-Assisted Instruction. Attitudes of teachers and correlates, Perspectives in education. 2002; 18(4):235-242.

82. Jyoti Tare. A Study of the Effectiveness of Branching Variety of Programmed Instructional Material as Diagnostic and Remedial Tool in Chemistry for Secondary Classes in Jabalpur DivisionCASE, The M.S. University of Baroda, Vadodara, 2001.

83. Kadhiravan S. Conducted a study on Effectiveness of computer Assisted Instruction in relation to students use. Un published M.Phil in education dissertation, 1999.

84. Kanmani M, Annaraja P. Influence of self-esteem and awareness of ICT on Academic Achievement of M.Ed. students. EDUTRACKS, June. 2009; 8(10):36-39.

85. Kante C, Savani V. e-Learning - The New Frontier in the Developing World. Tech Know Logia, 2003, 5(1).

86. Kay Stables, Richard Kimbell. Technology Education in South Africa: Evaluating an Innovative Pilot Project. Research in Science Education. 2001; 31(1):71-90.

87. Kerr ST. Lever and fulcrum: Educational technology in teachers' thought and practice. Teachers College Record. 1991; 93:114-136.

88. Kimbell R, Perry D. Design and technology in a knowledge economy. London: Engineering Council, 2001.

89. Kirkup G, Kirkwood A. Information and communications technologies (ICT) in higher education teaching-a tale of gradualism rather than

revolution. Learning, Media and Technology. 2005; 30(2):185-199.

90. Kirsti Ala-Mutka. Problems in learning and teaching programming- a literature study for developing visualizations in the Codewitz-Minerva project, Institute of Software Systems, Tampere University of Technology, Finland. Codewitz Needs Analysis Literature Study, 2009.

91. Knapper C. The challenge of educational technology. The International Journal for Academic Development. 2001; 6(2):93-95.

92. Koschmann TD *et al.* Using technology to assist in realizing effective learning and instruction: A principled approach to the use of computers in collaborative learning. Journal of the Learning Sciences. 1994; 3:227-264.

93. Kromhout O, Butzin S. (Fall). Integrating computers into the elementary school curriculum: An evaluation of nine Project child model schools. Journal of Research on Computing in Education. 1993; 26:55

94. Kulik C, Kulik J. Effectiveness of computer-based instruction: An updated analysis. Computers in Human Behavior. 1991; 7:75-94.

95. Kulik J *et al.* Effectiveness of computer-based education in elementary schools. Computers in Human Behavior, (ERIC Document Reproduction Service No. EJ 327 015). 1985; 7:59-74.

96. Kumar KL. Science and Technology Courses via E-Learning: An African Scenario with Lessons from South East Asia. International Journal on E-learning. 2002; 1(3):65-70.

97. Kumar N. prospects and problems in the use of Educational Media case study of an agricultural university Indian Educational Review. 1998; 34(2):90-98.

98. Lanier J, Little J. Research in teacher education. In M. C. Wittrock (Ed.). Handbook of research on teaching. New York: Macmillan, 1986, 527-569.

99. Laura Czerniewicz. Cape of Storms or Cape of Good Hope? Educational Technology in a Changing Environment. British Journal of Educational Technology. 2004; 35(2):145-158.

100. Leary T. An interpersonal diagnosis of personality. New York: Macmillan, 1957.

101. Lunenberg M, Korthagen F, Swennen A. The teacher educator as a role model. Teaching and Teacher Education. 2007; 23:586-601.

102.Mala Sharma, Sumar Sharma. Attitude of science teachers toards project method. EDUTRACKS, Febrauary. 2009; 8(6):40-43.

103.Mandi Axmann, Wiida Fourie, William Duncan Papo. Adding Net Value: The Nature of Online Education at a South African Residential Institution. Educational Media International. 2002; 39(3-4):267-73.

104.Manoharan M. Studied the relative effectiveness of print media Ph.D Education. T.N. Agricultural University, V.Survey of research education, 1988, 1379.

105.Margaret Wallace. An investigation into copyright concerns as a barrier to the widespread development of e-learning practice within Scottish further education colleges. Information & Communications Technology Law. 2006; 15:79-119.

106.Maria Athaide. A Study of the Effectiveness of the Training Program conducted by Intel-India for Secondary School Teachers Abstracts CASE, The M.S. University of Baroda, Vadodara - 390 002, 2005.

107.Marx RW *et al.* Enacting project-based science. Elementary School Journal, 1997; 97:341-58.

108.Mayer M, Scorborough D. The state networking report: Progress, policies, and partnerships bring Internet connectivity to K-12 schools. Austin, TX: Southwest Educational Development Laboratory, 1997.

109.Mc Kenzee, Frank Hubert, Mc Auleng. Students and teachers perception perception of the relationship among the utilization of school based (k-12) Educational Technology, students achievement and improved students learning Dissertation Abstract International. 2000; 62:58A.

110.McCracken J. Design-The creative soul of technology. In E.Martin (Ed.), Technology education for the 21st century: 49th Yearbook, Council on Technology Teacher Education. Peoria, Il: Glencoe/McGraw-Hill, 2000, 85-90.

111.McKenzie J. The wired classroom: Creating technology enhanced student-centered learning environments. From Now On, The Educational Technology Journal, 7 [Online], 1998. Available: http://www.fno.org/mar98/flotilla.html

112.McMahon T, Knuth R. Literature review: Administrative issues related to technology integration. Belleville, MI: Great Lakes Collaborative, 1995.

113.Mergendoller JR. Sifting the hype: What research says about technology and learning. Principal. 1997; 76:12-14.

114.Michelle Selinger. Cultural and Pedagogical Implications of a Global E-learning Programme. Cambridge Journal of Education. 2004; 34(2):223-239.

115.Mike Savage, Prem Naidoo. Popularisation of Science and Technology Education: Some Case Studies from Africa. Commonwealth Secretariat, London (England), 2002, 270.

116.Miller P. TV in the Classroom: Still Good as Gold. February 1998. KNPB Online. Retrieved December 30, 1998, 2003. From www.knpb.org/commentsabouteducation/199802. asp.

117.Minishi-Majanja, Mabel K. Information and Communication Technologies in Library and Information Science Education in South Africa. Mousaion. 2004; 22(2):150-71.

118.Moersch C. Computer efficiency: Measuring the instructional use of technology. Learning and Leading with Technology. 1996-97; 24:52-56.

119.Monica Landoni, Paloma Diaz. E-education: Design and Evaluation for Teaching and Learning. Journal of Digital Information, 2003, 3(4).

120.Niemiec RP *et al*. Comparing the cost-effectiveness of tutoring and computer-based instruction. Journal of Educational Computing Research. 1989; 5:395-407.

121.Nirmal Sabharwal. (Aug) Conducted study on "Innovations in Teaching Technology, 1996.

122.Nishi Jain. A Study of IGNOU Teleconferencing for Distance Learners CASE, The M.S. University of Baroda, Vadodara, 2002.

123.Northwest Regional Educational Laboratory. (Spring). Taking off: A teacher's guide to technology. Northwest Education. 1998; 3:3.

124.Novak DI, Knowles JG. Beginning elementary teachers' use of computers in classroom instruction. Action in Teacher Education. 1991; 13:43-51.

125.O'Hagan C. Embedding ubiquitous use of educational technology: is it possible, do we want it and, if so, how do we achieve it? Educational Technology & Society. 1999; 2(4):19-22.

126.Oakland County (MI) Schools. Teaching and learning with technology (Evaluation Report). Pontiac, MI: Author. (ERIC Document Reproduction Service No. ED 339 362), 1991.

127.Obajemu AS, Ibegwam A. A Survey of Librarians' Attitudes to Training

Programmes on ICTApplication to Cataloguing and Classification Workshops in Nigeria. African Journal of Library, Archives & Information Science. 2006; 16(1):19-27.

128.Pascal Zachary G. A Program for Africa's Computer People. Issues in Science and Technology. 2003; 19(3):79-85.

129.Paul Tiyambe, Zeleza Adebayo Olukoshi. African Universities in the Twenty-first Century. Volume II: Knowledge and Society, 2004, 350.

130.Philip Uys M, Paul Nleya, Molelu GB. Technological Innovation and Management Strategies for Higher Education in Africa: Harmonizing Reality and Idealism. Educational Media International. 2004; 41(1):67-80.

131.Philip Uys A. Syntagm of networked educational management: case study-University of Botswana. Campus-Wide Information Systems. 2004; 21(1):22-28.

132.Poirot JL. Assessment and evaluation of technology in education: The teacher as researcher. Computing Teacher. 1992; 20:9-10.

133.Poirot JL, Knezek GA. Experimental designs for determining the effectiveness of technology in education. Computing Teacher. 1992; 20:8-9.

134.Pullias D. The future is... beyond modular. Technology Teacher, (ERIC Document Reproduction Service No. EJ 542 160). 1997; 56:28-29.

135.Quigley BL, Nyquist JD. Using video technology to provide feedback to students in performance courses. Communication Education. 1992; 41:324-334.

136.Rajamony N. Conducted a study on 'Recent development in educational technology. Unpublished master in education dissertation, 1989.

137.Rakesh Pardeshi. A study of the relative effectiveness of CAI and CAIPI in learning Trigonometry by English medium students of Standard IX of Baroda City Abstracts of Research Studies Conductedby Teacher Education Institutions in India Dr. Goel, Chhaya Goel, RL Madhavi CASE, The M.S. University of Baroda, Vadodara-390 002, 2005.

138.Ramachandra Reddy B. Educational Technology, Tirupathi: Director of Distance Education, S.V. University, 1998.

139.Ramakrishna A. Teaching Aptitude of students of B.Ed Colleges. EDUTRACKS, October. 2008; 8(2):32-35.

140.Rasinen A. Developing technology education; In search of curriculum elements for Finnish general education schools. Jyväskylän yliopisto. Jyväskylä studies in education, psychology and social research, 2000, 171.

141.Reeta Chopra, Radhakanta Gartia. Accountablity of secondary school teachers in relation to their occupationasl stress ..7, EDUTRACKS, March. 2009; 8(7):41-43.

142.Reeves TC. The impact of Media and Technology in Schools: A Research report prepared for the Bertelsmann Foundation. Retrieved December 29, 1998, 2003. From:http://www.athensacademy.org/ instruct/media_tech/reeveso.html.

143.Riffel J, Levin B. Schools coping with the impact of information technology. Educational Management and Administration. 1997; 25:51-64.

144.Ringstaff C, Kelly L. The learning return on our educational technology investment: a review of findings from research. Wested RTEC, 2002. Retrieved from: http://ww.ecs.org.

145.Sahaya Mary R, Paul Raj I. Scientific Attitude of Upper Primary students towards science learning. EDUTRACKS, October. 2008; 8(2):29-31.

146.Sampath K, Pannirselvam A, Santhanam S. Introduction to Educational Techinology; Sterling publishers Pvt. Ltd; L-10; Green Park Extension, New Delhi, 1981.

147.Satoru Fujitani, Bhattacharya Madhumita, Kanji Akahori. ICT Implementation and Online Learning in Japan. Educational Technology. 2002; 43(3):33-7.

148.Scardamalia M, Bereiter C. Higher levels of agency for children in knowledge building: A challenge for the design of new knowledge media. Journal of the Learning Sciences, 1991; 37-68.

149.Scardamalia M, Bereiter C, McLean R, Swallow J, Woodruff E. (January). Computer-supported intentional learning environments. Journal of Educational Computing Research, 1989, 51-68.

150.Secules T *et al.* Creating schools for thought. Educational Leadership. (ERIC Document Reproduction Service No. ED 540 882). 1997; 54:56-60.

151.Sevilay SAHIN, Esen TURAN. The effects and uses of educational technology in learning and teaching January Kastamonu Education Journal, 2009, 17(1).

152.Shade DD. (Ed.). Children and computers abstracts. Journal of Computing in Childhood Education. 1992; 3:97-100.

153.Shaheeda Jaffer Dick, Ng'ambi Laura Czerniewicz. The role of ICTs in higher education in South Africa: one strategy for addressing teaching and learning challenges" University of Cape Town University of Cape Town University of Cape Town, 2009. sjaffer@ched.uct.ac.zalcz@ched.uct.ac.za.

154.Shanti S. Conducted a study of technologies of teaching in schools. Unpublished master in education dissertation, 2001-2002.

155.Sharma AR. Educational Technology; Vinod Pustak Mandir, Dr. Rangaraya Raghava Marg; Agra-2, 1992.

156.Sheela G. knowledge of information and communication, 2006.

157.Shelley Wepner B, Liging Tao, Nancy Ziomek M. Three Teacher Educators' Perspectives about the Shifting Responsibilities of Infusing Technology into the Curriculum. Action in Teacher Education. 2003; 24(4):53-63.

158.Sivin-Kachala J, Bialo ER. (Winter). Educational technology, teaching, and the development of complex skills. Edutopia. 1994-1995; 2(2):9-10.

159.Sneha Joshi M, Pushpanadham K, Anjali Khirwadkar. Knowledge Management through E-Learning:An Emerging Trend in the Indian Higher Education System. International Journal on E-Learning. 2002; 1(3):47-54.

160.Solachi T. Conducted a study on availability and utilization of Educational Technology in the Higher Secondary Schools of districts of Pasumpson, Tehvar, Thirumagan in Tamil Nadu state, survey of Research in Education, 1991.

161.Steketee C. Integrating ICT as an integral teaching and learning tool into preservice teacher training courses. Issues in Educational Research. 2005; 15(10):101-112.

162.Sumangala V, Ushadevi VK. Role Conflict, Attitude towards teaching profession and job satisfaction as predictors of success in teaching". EDUTRACKS, May. 2009; 8(9):25-29.

163.Sunderberg, Cheryl White. Studied impact of different communication technology to support professional development of teaching science dissertation abstract international. 2000, 2001; 61(12):4666.

164. Susan McKenney. Technology for Curriculum And Teacher Development: Software To Help Educators Learn While Designing Teacher Guides. Journal of Research on Technology in Education. 2005; 38(2):167-9.

165. Suwanna Ruttanathummatee. Effectiveness of Computer Assisted Instruction for Primary School Students: An Experimental Study iCASE, The M.S. University of Baroda, Vadodara, 2004.

166. Technology and attitude towards teaching ICT among teacher educators. Experimental in Education. 2004; XXXIV(8):157-164.

167. Thatte CH. An Experimental Study of the Relative Effectiveness of Programmed Learning andLearning Through Audio Visual Aids with reference to certain selected topics fromthe syllabus of Science for Std. V to VII in Greater Bombay CASE, The M.S. University of Baroda, Vadodara - 390 002, 1998.

168. The influence of system characteristics on e-learning use. Computers & Education. 2006; 47(2):222-44.

169. The State of the Art of Distance Education in SEAMEO. Member Countries. SEAMEO Forum. 1995; 2(2):5-12.

170. Therese Laferriere, Mary Lamon, Carol KK Chan. Emerging E-Trends and Models in Teacher Education and Professional Development. Teaching Education (Columbia, S.C.). 2006; 17(1):75-90.

171. Tim Unwin. Toward a Framework for the Use of ICT in Teacher Training in Africa. Open Learning. 2005; 20(2):113-129.

172. Usha Rani P. Role of educational technology in teaching-learning of English language in higher education. Un published master in education dissertation, 1999-2000.

173. Usha Sri V. Use of technology by teachers. Un published master in education dissertation, 1999-2000.

174. Van Dusen L, Worthen B. Computer-based integrated learning systems: Research and theory. International Journal of Educational Research, 1994, 13-52.

175. Vandana Mehra, Dilli Raj Newa. School teachers Attitude towards information and communication technology (ICT), EDUTRACKS, Feb. 2009; 8(6):25-31.

176. Vasanthi A, Hema S. effectiveness of teaching chemistry for I year B.E. students through Computer Assisted Instruction (CAI) Journalals of Educational research and Extension, 2003, 40(2).

177. Wagner AD. IT and Education for the Poorest of the Poor: Constraints, Possibilities, and Principles. TechKnowLogia, July/August, 2001, 48-50.

178. Watson G, Proctor R, Finger G, Lang W. Auditing the ICT experiencesof teacher education undergraduates. Australian Educational Computing. 2004; 19(1):3-10.

179. William Horton, Katherine Horton. E-learning Tools and Technologies: A consumer's guide for trainers, teachers, educators, and instructional designers. John Wiley & Sons. 2003, 592.

180. Wulf. Emphasized the importance of edcuational technology K-12 classroom in America, 2000. http://www.wested.org/ techpolicy/ recapproach.html.

181. Yadav Kusum. Development of an IT enabled Instructional Package for Teaching English medium students of Vadodara city The M.S. University of Baroda, Vadodara-390 002, 2004.

182. Yashobanta Samal. Effectiveness of the School Broadcast Programmes of All India Radio (AIR) andEducational Television (ETV) Programme s of Doordarshan with reference to school achievement of the learners CASE, The M.S. University of Baroda, Vadodara-390 002, 2000. File:///D|/research %20abstracts /drg1.htm 11/20/2006.

APPENDIX - A

DRAVIDIAN UNIVERSITY

Department of education

KUPPAM

PRELIMINARY FORM OF THE CHECKLIST CUM RATING QUESTIONNAIRE

Topic: A STUDY OF TEACHING – LEARNING PROBLEMS IN EDUCATIONAL TECHNOLOGY AT B.ED LEVEL.

Guide: Dr. G. Ranga Swamy **Scholar: Chavan Vijaya Kumar**

M.A., M.Ed., Ph.D. **M.Sc., M.Ed., M.Phil**

1. **Name of the Teacher Educator** :
2. **Sex** : **Male/Female**
3. **Age** :
4. **Qualification** :
   a. **Academic** :
   b. **Professional** :
5. **Name of the college and Place** :
6. **Management** : **Govt/Aided/Un-Aided**
7. **Area** : **Urban/ Rural**
8. **Socio Economic Status** : **Rich/Middle/Poor**
9. **Methodologies handling** :
   a.
   b.
10. **Total Experience at B. Ed level**

Instructions

In the given questionnaire, there are some statements related to the problem in teaching/learning education technology at B. Ed level. After reading the statement if it is suited to your problem, then put a (✓) mark in the first column yes/no. Then again the other column indicates the intensity of your problem rating highly, moderately and Low. Based upon your intensity put (✓) in any one of the column that suits you. If the statement is not applicable you put (✕) mark in the first column. Don't leave any statement blank.

S. No	Statement/Problem	Yes/No	If yes High/moderate/Low
1.	Are you facing problem to teach the subject in regional language?	Yes/no	If yes High/moderate/Low
2.	While prepararing for the class, contents cannot be digested at once.	Yes/no	If yes High/moderate/Low
3.	Technology apparatus cannot be used appropriately during technology training process.	Yes/no	If yes High/moderate/Low
4.	Problems in using right terminology is often observed	Yes/no	If yes High/moderate/Low
5	Problem in clarifying the doubts relating to the subject.	Yes/no	If yes High/moderate/Low
6	Do you feel difficult to teach computers due to computer knowledge?	Yes/no	If yes High/moderate/Low
7	Lack of awareness in teaching the subject at the student level.	Yes/no	If yes High/moderate/Low
8	Do you feel difficulty in teaching Action Research topic in Educational Technology?	Yes/no	If yes High/moderate/Low
9	Do you feel difficulty in teaching DOS commands and programmes	Yes/no	If yes High/moderate/Low
10	There is Problem in using A.V. aids .	Yes/no	If yes High/moderate/Low
11	No refreshing courses for the subject lecturers regarding A.V aids.	Yes/no	If yes High/moderate/Low
12	Physical Science methodology teacher can teach Education Technology better than other subject teachers.	Yes/no	If yes High moderate/Low
13	There are Problems in teaching some topics regarding latest technology.	Yes/no	If yes High/moderate/Low
14	Teachers undergo Problems in teaching for both practical and theory effectively.	Yes/no	If yes High/moderate/Low
15	During workshop are you guiding that student teachers to prepare teaching learning material of low or no cost.	Yes/no	If yes High/moderate/Low
16	Problem with lack of resource of equipment in B. Ed Colleges.	Yes/no	If yes High/moderate/Low
17	Proportionate teaching aids are not used in respect to theory.	Yes/no	If yes High/moderate/Low
18	Non-availability of adequate equipment in lab.	Yes/no	If yes

			High/moderate/Low
19	There is lack of equipment according to the student strength (ratio).	Yes/no	If yes High/moderate/Low
20	Did you train your students how to download technology related from the internet	Yes/no	If yes High/moderate/Low
21	Lack of idea in teaching micro-teaching skills .	Yes/no	If yes High/moderate/Low
22	In most of the cases micro-teaching cycle process is not followed.	Yes/no	If yes High/moderate/Low
23	Are you using multimedia approach in the classroom teaching.	Yes/no	If yes High/moderate/Low
24	Are you making the students to prepare a lesson plan by computer	Yes/no	If yes High/moderate/Low
25	Even if we use the microteaching cycle, time is not sufficient for the one year course.	Yes/no	If yes High/moderate/Low
26	During the observation of Micro teaching lesson, teacher-educator does not have an idea on classroom interaction	Yes/no	If yes High/moderate/Low
27	Even if we have an idea on classroom interaction, time is not sufficient to teach all skills effectively	Yes/no	If yes High/moderate/Low
28	Do you feel any problem in teaching Dale's Cone of experience by appropriate Teaching Learning Material?	Yes/no	If yes High/moderate/Low
29	Skilled teachers are not available for teaching the microteaching lessons.	Yes/no	If yes High/moderate/Low
30	For the feedback process in microteaching, required no. of audio-visual equipment is not available.	Yes/no	If yes High/moderate/Low
31	Do you have right experience to rate the scale of micro-teaching components?	Yes/no	If yes High/moderate/Low
32	Very few microteaching skills are taught in the class due to not knowing them properly.	Yes/no	If yes High/moderate/Low
33	Have you suggested your student to use Video Cam for the feedback of Micro Teaching skills.	Yes/no	If Yes High/moderate/Low
34	Most of the teachers while teaching the skills they are not able to perform proportionate movements related to the skill before students	Yes/no	If yes High/moderate/Low
35	If the right teacher performs right skill movements, the student teacher feels that it is	Yes/no	If yes High/moderate/Low

	an entertainment programme.		
36	To develop a skill we require minimum 36 minutes. But time does not permit the concerned lecturer to complete the cycle.	Yes/no	If yes High/moderate/Low
37	Due to lack of idea on technology, the teacher is not able to teach about the regarding projected and non- projected teaching aids effectively.	Yes/no	If yes High/moderate/Low
38	Most of the technology lecturers have less command on methodology content.	Yes/no	If yes High/moderate/Low
39	The educational technology lecturers cannot satisfy the social science students regarding the science related topics.	Yes/no	If yes High/moderate/Low
40	There is no positive response from the student teacher when they are taught by a qualified technology teacher	Yes/no	If yes High/moderate/Low
41	Due to lack of basic knowledge on A.V.aids, the teacher educator faces problems in teaching the subject.	Yes/no	If yes High/moderate/Low
42	Most of the teacher educators are confused by the terms hardware and software.	Yes/no	If yes High/moderate/Low
43	Have you projected any new ideas in preparing Teaching Learning Material other than Thermocool.	Yes/no	If Yes High/moderate/Low
44	Do you feel it difficult in teaching class room interaction like FAICS, VICS etc.	Yes/no	If Yes High/moderate/Low
45	Because of short duration of the course, the teacher may have maximum problems on analyzing the psychology of the students.	Yes/no	If yes High/moderate/Low
46	If the micro skills are not taught properly it may affect the macro teaching in methodologies.	Yes/no	If yes High/moderate/Low
47	Do you find it difficult in teaching the concept of programming learning.	Yes/no	If yes High/moderate/Low
48	Do you difficulty teaching the concept of Mathematics.	Yes/no	If yes High/moderate/Low
49	Have you taught the computer assisted instruction (CAI) and programmed instruction (PI) without any problem?	Yes/no	If yes High/moderate/Low
50	In most cases, teachers are not following the principles of demonstration.	Yes/no	If yes High/moderate/Low

APPENDIX - B

DRAVIDIAN UNIVERSITY

DEPARTMENT OF EDUCATION

KUPPAM

Topic: A STUDY OF TEACHING – LEARNING PROBLEMS IN EDUCATIONAL TECHNOLOGY AT B.ED LEVEL.

Guide: Dr. G. Ranga Swamy **Scholar: Chavan Vijaya Kumar**

M.A., M.Ed., Ph.D. **M.Sc., M.Ed., M.Phil**

1. **Name of the Teacher Educator** :
2. **Sex** : **Male / Female Age**
3. **Qualification** :
   i. **Academic** :
   ii. **Professional** :
4. **Name of the college and Place** :
5. **Management** : **Govt / Aided / Un-Aided**
6. **Area** : **Urban/Rural**
7. **Socio Economic Status** : **Rich / Middle / Poor**
8. **Methodologies handling** :
   i. a.
   ii. b.
9. **Total Experience at B. Ed level** :

Instructions

In the given questionnaire, there are some statements related to the problem in teaching/learning education technology at B. Ed level. After reading the statement if it is suited to your problem, then put a (✓) mark in the first column yes/no. Then again the other column indicates the intensity of your problem rating highly, moderately and Low. Based upon your intensity put (✓) in any one of the column that suits you. If the statement is not applicable you put (✕) mark in the first column. Don't leave any statement blank.

S. No	Statement/Problem	Yes/No	If Yes
			High/Moderate/Low
1.	Are you facing problem to teach the subject in regional language?	Yes/no	If yes High/moderate/Low
2.	While prepararing for the class, contents cannot be digested at once.	Yes/no	If yes
			High/moderate/Low
3.	Technology apparatus cannot be used appropriately during technology training process.	Yes/no	If yes
			High/moderate/Low
4.	Problems in using right terminology is often observed	Yes/no	If yes
			High/moderate/Low
5.	Problem in clarifying the doubts relating to the subject.	Yes/no	If yes
			High/moderate/Low
6	Do you feel difficult to teach computers due to computer knowledge?	Yes/no	If yes
			High/moderate/Low
7	Lack of awareness in teaching the subject at the student level.	Yes/no	If yes
			High/moderate/Low
8	Do you feel difficulty in teaching Action Research topic in Educational Technology?	Yes/no	If yes
			High/moderate/Low
9	There is Problem in using A.V. aids .	Yes/no	If yes
			High/moderate/Low
10	No refreshing courses for the subject lecturers regarding A.V aids.	Yes/no	If yes
			High/moderate/Low
11	There are Problems in teaching some topics regarding latest technology.	Yes/no	If yes
			High/moderate/Low
12	Teachers undergo Problems in teaching for both practical and theory effectively.	Yes/no	If yes
			High/moderate/Low
13	Problem with lack of resource of equipment in B. Ed Colleges.	Yes/no	If yes
			High/moderate/Low
14	Proportionate teaching aids are not used in respect to theory.	Yes/no	If yes
			High/moderate/Low
15	Non-availability of adequate equipment in lab.	Yes/no	If yes
			High/moderate/Low
16	There is lack of equipment according to the student strength (ratio).	Yes/no	If yes
			High/moderate/Low
17	Lack of idea in teaching micro-teaching skills.	Yes/no	If yes
			High/moderate/Low
18	In most of the cases micro-teaching cycle process is not followed.	Yes/no	f yes
			High/moderate/Low

19	Even if we use the microteaching cycle, time is not sufficient for the one year course.	Yes/no	If yes High/moderate/Low
20	During the observation of Micro teaching lesson, teacher-educator does not have an idea on classroom interaction.	Yes/no	If yes High/moderate/Low
21	Even if we have an idea on classroom interaction, time is not sufficient to teach all skills effectively.	Yes/no	If yes High/moderate/Low
22	Skilled teachers are not available for teaching the microteaching lessons.	Yes/no	If yes High/moderate/Low
23	For the feed back process in microteaching, required no. of audio-visual equipment is not available.	Yes/no	If yes High/moderate/Low
24	Do you have right experience to rate the scale of micro-teaching components?	Yes/no	If yes High/moderate/Low
25	Very few microteaching skills are taught in the class due to not knowing them properly.	Yes/no	If yes High/moderate/Low
26	Most of the teachers while teaching the skills they are not able to perform proportionate movements related to the skill before students	Yes/no	If yes High/moderate/Low
27	If the right teacher performs right skill movements, the student teacher feels that it is an entertainment programme.	Yes/no	If yes High/moderate/Low
28	To develop a skill we require minimum 36 minutes. But time does not permit the concerned lecturer to complete the cycle.	Yes/no	If yes High/moderate/Low
29	Due to lack of idea on technology, the teacher is not able to teach about the regarding projected and non- projected teaching aids effectively.	Yes/no	If yes High/moderate/Low
30	ost of the technology lecturers have less command on methodology content.	Yes/no	If yes High/moderate/Low
31	The educational technology lecturers cannot satisfy the social science students regarding the science related topics.	Yes/no	If yes High/moderate/Low
32	There is no positive response from the student teacher when they are taught by a qualified technology teacher	Yes/no	If yes High/moderate/Low
33	Due to lack of basic knowledge on A.V.aids, the teacher educator faces problems in teaching the subject.	Yes/no	If yes High/moderate/Low
34	Most of the teacher educators are confused by the terms hardware and software.	Yes/no	If yes High/moderate/Low
35	Do you feel it difficult in teaching class room	Yes/no	If Yes

	interaction like FAICS, VICS etc.		High/moderate/Low
36	Because of short duration of the course, the teacher may have maximum problems on analyzing the psychology of the students.	Yes/no	If yes High/moderate/Low
37	If the micro skills are not taught properly it may affect the macro teaching in methodologies.	Yes/no	If yes High/moderate/Low
38	Do you find it difficult in teaching the concept of programming learning.	Yes/no	If yes High/moderate/Low
39	Have you taught the computer assisted instruction (CAI) and programmed instruction (PI) without any problem?	Yes/no	If yes High/moderate/Low
40	In most cases, teachers are not following the principles of demonstration.	Yes/no	If yes High/moderate/Low

APPENDIX - C

DRAVIDIAN UNIVERSITY

KUPPAM

Department of education

PRELIMINARY FORM OF THE CHECKLIST CUM RATING QUESTIONNAIRE

Topic: A STUDY OF TEACHING – LEARNING PROBLEMS IN EDUCATIONAL TECHNOLOGY AT B.ED LEVEL.

Guide: Dr. G. Ranga Swamy **Scholar: Chavan Vijaya Kumar**

M.A., M Ed., Ph.D. M. Sc., M.Ed., M. Phil.

1. **Name of the student Teacher** :
2. **Sex** : **Male/Female**
3. **Age** :
4. **Qualification** :
    a. **Academic** :
    b. **Professional** :
5. **Name of the college & Place** :
6. **Management** : **Govt/Aided/Un-Aided**
7. **Area** : **Urban/ Rural**
8. **Socio Economic Status** : **Rich/Middle/Poor**
9. **Methodologies opted** :
    a.
    b.

Instructions

In the given questionnaire, there are some statements related to the problem in teaching/learning education technology at B.Ed level. After reading the statement if it is suited to your problem, then put a (✓) mark in the first column yes/no. Then again the other column indicates the intensity of your problem rating High/moderate/less. Based upon your intensity put (✓) in any one of the column that suits you. If the statement is not applicable you put (✕) mark in the first column. Don't leave any statement blank.

S. No	Statement/Problem	Yes/No	If yes
			High/moderate/less
1	Students are facing multi problems regarding language which is used by different lecturers who have come from different areas.	Yes/No	If yes High/moderate/less
2	Are you facing the problem in learning the B.Ed subject because it differs from the subjects at graduation within a short duration?		If yes High/moderate/less
3	There is a problem in learning the mechanism of hardware and software.	Yes/No	If yes High/moderate/less
4	There is a difficulty to learn DOS commands and programmes	Yes/No	If yes High/moderate/less
5	Science students are well capable in learning and operating the equipment of technology when compared to social students.	Yes/No	If yes High/moderate/less
6	Some contents are not understood because of wrong explanation by the teacher educator.	Yes/No	If yes High/moderate/less
7	If your teachers are not able to clarify your doubts do you feel that educational technology is a difficult subject	Yes/No	If yes High/moderate/less
8	Do you feel any problem, when your mates are disturbing the classroom during a good lecture?	Yes/No	If yes High/moderate/less
9	Lecturers are not interested in operating the laboratory equipment.	Yes/No	If yes High/moderate/less
10	Are you not able to adverse with subject computers.	Yes/No	If yes High/moderate/less
11	Some of the lecturers are not able to operate the technology apparatus in classroom/lab.	Yes/No	If yes High/moderate/less
12	There is a problem of learning the theory in proportionate to practical in educational technology.	Yes/No	If yes High/moderate/less
13	Due to over load of syllabus and non - availability of duration, it is difficult for you to learn educational technology.	Yes/No	If yes High/moderate/less
14	Some of the teachers do not know about the microteaching skills.	Yes/No	If yes High/moderate/less
15	Because of huge curriculum I am not able to follow all the skills of microteaching.	Yes/No	If yes High/moderate/less
16	Do you feel difficulty in learning educational technology because unqualified and unrelated subject teachers teach the subject?	Yes/No	If yes High/moderate/less

17	Do you feel difficult in learning the difference between the different classroom interaction like FAICS,VICS etc.	Yes/No	If yes High/moderate/less
18	Have you any problem in learning the concept of programme learning?	Yes/No	If yes High/moderate/less
19	Have you any problem in learning the concept of Mathetics	Yes/No	If yes High/moderate/less
20	Have you any difficulty in understanding the topic system approach in educational technology?	Yes/No	If yes High/moderate/less
21	The usage of technology regularly in classroom will become a chance to convert as enjoyment	Yes/No	If yes High/moderate/less
22	Is computer assisted instruction (CAI) and programmed instruction (PI) are taught by your teacher well?	Yes/No	If yes High/moderate/less
23	Does your institution has sufficient computers and internet facility?	Yes/No	Yes/No High/moderate/less
24	Is your institution having sufficient number of technical persons to operate the technological equipments	Yes/No	If yes High/moderate/less
25	Does your institution provide you in learning the internet and multimedia approach often?	Yes/No	If yes High/moderate/less
26	Is your institution providing systematic audio lab and language laboratory?	Yes/No	If yes High/moderate/less
27	Are you facing problem with Educational technology terminology?	Yes/No	If yes High/moderate/less
28	Do you have any difficulty in understanding the topic action research	Yes/No	If yes High/moderate/less
29	Do you memorize the hierarchy of steps in Dale's cone of experience?	Yes/No	If yes High/moderate/less
30	Have you learn all skills in micro teaching	Yes/No	If yes High/moderate/less
31	Is your lecturers using multimedia approach in the classroom teaching	Yes/No	If yes High/moderate/less
32	Are you facing any problem in learning the computer subject (M.S.office) in educational technology?	Yes/No	If yes High/moderate/less
33	Educational technology cannot understand at once	Yes/No	If yes High/moderate/less
34	My lecturers are guiding and giving practice in operating hardware equipment.		

35	Does your teacher welcome your ideas in learning software development?	Yes/No	If yes High/moderate/less
36	Are you having a separate computer instructor to operate and teach the computer subject?	Yes/No	If yes High/moderate/less
37	Are you having educational technology lab & computer lab separately?	Yes/No	If yes High/moderate/less
38	During your microteaching, did your teacher make it compulsory to follow the microteaching cycle?	Yes/No	If yes High/moderate/less
39	Problems in using A.V. Aids	Yes/No	If yes High/moderate/less
40	To develop a skill we require minimum 36 minutes. But according the time table time is not permitting for a student teacher to complete the cycle	Yes/No	If yes High/moderate/less
41	Is microteaching helpful to you in promoting your teaching skills?	Yes/No	If yes High/moderate/less
42	Skilled teacher are not available for teaching the micro teaching	Yes/No	If yes High/moderate/less
43	Are you facing problem in operating projected and non projected teaching aid during your internships?	Yes/No	If yes High/moderate/less
44	Are you having sufficient material for learning Educational Technology?	Yes/No	If Yes High/moderate/less
45	Most of the student teachers while teaching the skills they are not able to perform proportionately	Yes/No	If Yes High/moderate/less

APPENDIX - D

DRAVIDIAN UNIVERSITY

DEPARTMENT OF EDUCATION

KUPPAM

Topic: A STUDY OF TEACHING – LEARNING PROBLEMS IN EDUCATIONAL TECHNOLOGY AT B.ED LEVEL.

Guide: Dr. G. Ranga Swamy **Scholar: Chavan Vijaya Kumar**

M.A., M Ed., Ph.D. **M. Sc., M.Ed., M.Phil.**

1. **Name of the student Teacher** :
2. **Sex** : **Male / Female**
3. **Age** :
4. **Qualification** :
   a. **Academic** :
   b. **Professional** :
5. **Name of the college & Place** :
6. **Management** : **Govt/Aided/Un-Aided**
7. **Area** : **Urban/Rural**
8. **Socio Economic Status** : **Rich/Middle/Poor**
9. **Methodologies opted** :
   a.
   b.

Instructions

In the given questionnaire, there are some statements related to the problem in teaching/learning education technology at B.Ed level. After reading the statement if it is suited to your problem, then put a (✓) mark in the first column yes/no. Then again the other column indicates the intensity of your problem rating High/moderate/less. Based upon your intensity put (✓) in any one of the column that suits you. If the statement is not applicable you put (✕) mark in the first column. Don't leave any statement blank.

S. No	Statement/Problem	Yes/No	If yes High/moderate/less
1	Students are facing multi problems regarding language which is used by different lecturers who have come from different areas.	Yes/No	If yes High/moderate/less
2	Are you facing the problem in learning the B.Ed subject because it differs from the subjects at graduation within a short duration?	Yes/No	If yes High/moderate/less
3	There is a problem in learning the mechanism of hardware and software.	Yes/No	If yes High/moderate/less
4	Science students are well capable in learning and operating the equipment of technology when compared to social students.	Yes/No	If yes High/moderate/less
5	Some contents are not understood because of wrong explanation by the teacher educator.	Yes/No	If yes High/moderate/less
6	If your teachers are not able to clarify your doubts do you feel that educational technology is a difficult subject	Yes/No	If yes High/moderate/less
7	Do you feel any problem, when your mates are disturbing the classroom during a good lecture?	Yes/No	If yes High/moderate/less
8	Lecturers are not interested in operating the laboratory equipment.	Yes/No	If yes High/moderate/less
9	Are you not able to adverse with subject computers.	Yes/No	If yes High/moderate/less
10	Some of the lecturers are not able to operate the technology apparatus in classroom/lab.	Yes/No	If yes High/moderate/less
11	There is a problem of learning the theory in proportionate to practical in educational technology.	Yes/No	If yes High/moderate/less
12	Due to over load of syllabus and non - availability of duration, it is difficult for you to learn educational technology.	Yes/No	If yes High/moderate/less
13	Some of the teachers do not know about the microteaching skills.	Yes/No	If yes High/moderate/less
14	Because of huge curriculum I am not able to follow all the skills of microteaching.	Yes/No	If yes High/moderate/less
15	Do you feel difficulty in learning educational technology because unqualified and unrelated subject teachers teach the subject?	Yes/No	If yes High/moderate/less
16	Do you feel difficult in learning the difference between the different classroom interaction like FAICS,VICS etc.	Yes/No	If yes High/moderate/less

17	Have you any problem in learning the concept of programme learning?	Yes/No	If yes High/moderate/less
18	Have you any difficulty in understanding the topic system approach in educational technology?	Yes/No	If yes High/moderate/less
19	Is computer assisted instruction (CAI) and programmed instruction (PI) are taught by your teacher well?	Yes/No	If yes High/moderate/less
20	Does your institution has sufficient computers and internet facility?	Yes/No	If yes High/moderate/less
21	Does your institution provide you in learning the internet and multimedia approach often?	Yes/No	If yes High/moderate/less
22	Is your institution providing systematic audio lab and language laboratory?	Yes/No	If yes High/moderate/less
23	Are you facing problem with Educational technology terminology?	Yes/No	If yes High/moderate/less
24	Do you memorize the hierarchy of steps in Dale's cone of experience?	Yes/No	If yes High/moderate/less
25	Are you facing any problem in learning the computer subject (M.S.office) in educational technology?	Yes/No	If yes High/moderate/less
26	My lecturers are guiding and giving practice in operating hardware equipment.	Yes/No	If yes High/moderate/less
27	Does your teacher welcome your ideas in learning software development?	Yes/No	If yes High/moderate/less
28	Are you having a separate computer instructor to operate and teach the computer subject?	Yes/No	If yes High/moderate/less
29	Are you having educational technology lab & computer lab separately?	Yes/No	If yes High/moderate/less
30	During your microteaching, did your teacher make it compulsory to follow the microteaching cycle?	Yes/No	If yes High/moderate/less
31	Is microteaching helpful to you in promoting your teaching skills?	Yes/No	If yes High/moderate/less
32	Are you facing problem in operating projected and non projected teaching aid during your internships?	Yes/No	If yes High/moderate/less
33	Are you having sufficient material for learning Educational Technology?	Yes/No	If Yes High/moderate/less